T0288242

A Family Home

NELL RICHARDSON

An Auburn Book
Published in Association with The University of Alabama Press

A Family Home

A HISTORY OF THE PRESIDENT'S MANSION AT AUBURN UNIVERSITY

Manufactured in China

Designed by Todd Lape / Lape Designs

The paper on which this book is printed meets the minimum requirements of American National Standard for Information Science—Permanence of Paper for Printed Library Materials, ANSI Z39.48-1984.

Library of Congress Cataloging-in-Publication Data

Richardson, Nell, 1943–
A family home : a history of the president's mansion at Auburn University / Nell Richardson.
p. cm.
"An Auburn book."
Includes bibliographical references.
ISBN 978-0-8173-1617-4 (cloth : alk. paper) —
ISBN 978-0-8173-8059-5 (electronic) 1. Auburn University—Presidents—Homes and haunts—History. 2. Auburn University—Presidents—Biography. 3. Alabama Polytechnic Institute—Presidents—Homes and haunts—History. 4. Alabama Polytechnic Institute—Presidents—Biography. I. Title.
LD271.A6615R53 2008
378.761—dc22 2008015851

Contents

Preface

My husband, Ed Richardson, took up residence in the President's Home at Auburn University in January 2004. In the midst of a crisis over the president's authority that affected the University's accreditation, Ed had been asked to come to Auburn as interim president. At the end of a long career in public education that included his work with the state's universities, Ed accepted the job, confident that he would be able to initiate some positive changes at Auburn.

Ed had been on the Auburn board for more than eight years, and he had worked with many of the state's leaders as well as Governor Bob Riley to move the state forward. Ed believed that he could work with the governor and others to make improvements for Auburn University and the state of Alabama. He knew his stay would not be long, as the Southern Association of Colleges and Schools had mandated that Auburn make a national search for a permanent president as part of the renewal of their accreditation.

We did not sell our home in Montgomery, but I retired from teaching and came to Auburn to assist my husband with the very active life of a university president and his wife. In the President's Home I discovered a copy of the 1996 edition of *Auburn: A Pictorial History of the Loveliest Village,* by Mickey Logue and Jack Simms, and I started to look closely at the history of the once-small town and its football-famous university. Our family had lived in Auburn from 1982 to 1995, when Ed served as superintendent of Auburn schools. All four members of our family—Ed and I and our daughters Merit and Laura—had graduated from Auburn University.

In the preface of *A Pictorial History,* a picture of Samford Hall, taken in October 1995 just after Hurricane Opal had struck, stood out as an uncanny reflection of our circumstances in 1995 and in 2004. It reminded me of our personal upheaval in leaving Auburn in 1995 when Ed became superintendent of Alabama's public school system and of the storm of controversy Ed found on the Auburn campus when he served as trustee.

Over the years of our association with the city of Auburn and Auburn University, we had become acquainted with all of the families who have lived in the President's Home except for the Duncans. The Duncans were serving Auburn, then Alabama Polytechnic Institute (API), when Ed and I were children, but the Draughons, the Philpotts, the Funderburks, the Baileys, the Martins, and especially the Muses and Walkers were all people we had known in our adult lives.

Ed was an undergraduate when the Draughons were in the president's home, and the Philpotts were serving when Ed earned his doctorate. When the Funderburks came to Auburn from Auburn University at Montgomery (AUM) in 1980, we were moving to Montgomery where Ed would be associated with AUM. In 1982 when the Funderburks were at AU, we moved to Auburn for Ed's position as superintendent of Auburn schools.

We were still living in Auburn when the Martin administration (1984–92) ended. When the Muses arrived in the spring of 1992, we were among the first to meet them. The mayor of Auburn, Jan Dempsey, hosted a birthday party for the new minister of the Auburn Methodist Church, George Mathison, a tennis player and longtime friend of Ed's, and the Richardsons as well as the Muses attended.

To say that we knew Dr. Wilford Bailey, who served only one year as Auburn's president, is to join almost everyone in Auburn who admired and loved this man. Dr. Bailey was an Auburn institution in himself. He died in 2000, but we have come to know and love his wife, Kate, a wonderful lady who turned ninety in 2006.

We were grandparents when we moved into the President's Home in 2004, and it has been interesting to note that all of the nine presidents and their wives who have lived in the President's Home became grandparents during their residence. The y were not all in their sixties, as we were, when they came to the President's Home, however. The Draughons moved in with their early teenage children and stayed for seventeen years, growing up with the modern college and serving honorably as surrogate parents to nearly two decades of Auburn students. Following the Draughons in 1965, the Philpotts, both of whom were ordained ministers, filled up the President's Home with their four teenaged children.

The President's Home was the Philpott residence for fifteen years, and Dr. and Mrs. Philpott aged with the changing times and welcomed their first grandchildren to the President's Home before they retired and moved across town, leaving the "mansion" to the Funderburks. The Funderburks were not yet in their fifties when they came to the President's Home, but they too became grandparents during their service to Auburn University.

In the 1995 photo featured in *A Pictorial History*, Samford Hall was still standing among the debris and downed trees as it has through all the storms and challenges of its history. Built on the site of the "Old Main" of East Alabama (Methodist) Male College, this grand old hall housing the president's office would remain the same, I knew, after our time at Auburn was through. For all of the children and grandchildren who have known the President's Home at Auburn University, I have written this remembrance. I am certain that all the grandchildren who knew their grandparents as the President and First Lady of Auburn have been just as proud as our six-year-old granddaughter, Molly, who stood on the porch of the President's Home in December 2006 and greeted the guests at the Christmas open house with her favorite phrase of the day: "My papa's the seventeenth president of Auburn University."

My interest in writing about the President's Home at Auburn University began with the opening of a picture book, and it grew with the friendships and photos presented to me by the families of the eight First Ladies who lived in the President's Home before me. I became interested in the lives of these women who had come, as I had, to serve with their husbands (without a salary of their own), but with the

In the foyer of the President's Home, Nell Richardson approves of granddaughter Molly's Christmas greeting, December 2006. (Auburn University Photographic Services)

sense of duty presented to them by the president's position and with a respect for the mission of the institution they served. No doubt, we all have been honored to care for the President's Home for a time and content to leave it behind.

This book is dedicated to the Richardson grandchildren—Seth, Molly, and Gunnar—and to the grandchildren of the Duncans, Draughons, Philpotts, Funderburks, Baileys, Martins, Muses, and Walkers.

A Family Home

CHAPTER ONE

The Setting

The President's Home at Auburn University is set at the southern edge of the campus on an eleven-acre elevation that has always been part of Auburn's agricultural experiment heritage. The President's home was built by Auburn's first director of the Alabama Cooperative Extension Service and ninth president of Alabama Polytechnic Institute, Luther Duncan, who moved with his wife, Annie, into the new home for the president at Christmastime in 1939.

At Christmastime 2006 the President's Home at Auburn University had been standing on the site of an antebellum farmhouse for nearly seventy years. The white-columned, colonial home is located at 430 South College Street, but the house faces the campus. From College Street, the beauty of the President's Home and its setting are lost on the constant stream of passersby. From Samford Avenue, however, and especially from Mell Street, where the long, circular driveway to the house is clearly visible, the setting of the President's Home is impressive.

The President's Home at Auburn University stands overlooking the campus as it has since 1939. (Auburn University Photographic Services)

Before the Civil War, two colleges were located in Auburn: East Alabama Male College (the precursor of Auburn University), established in 1856, and Auburn Masonic Female College, founded in 1852. According to historians Mickey Logue and Jack Simms, both colleges helped to attract wealthy planters to the Auburn area. The women's college enrolled 106 students in the year of its founding and "was likely a factor in helping to bring East Alabama Male College to Auburn. The Civil War ended the prosperity of both institutions."[1]

The Darby/Duggar House was purchased by Alabama Agricultural and Mechanical College from J. B. Gay in March 1884. (Auburn University Special Collections)

In the 1950s the home of Professor John M. Darby, a chemist and pharmacist who taught chemistry to both the girls of Auburn Masonic Female College and the boys of East Alabama Male College stood where the President's Home now stands. In a small building near the site of the President's Home, Dr. Darby and his partner, W. H. C. Price, formulated a patent medicine that sold throughout the Southeast.

During the Civil War, "Prof. Darby's Prophylactic Fluid" aided the treatment of many ill and wounded soldiers brought to the "Old Main" building of EAMC. The administrative building of Auburn University, Samford Hall, located two blocks north of the President's Home on South College Street, was built in 1888 on this site. In 1861 Old Main lost its students to the Civil War effort and became known as the Texas Hospital, so named because of the financial support it received from the state of Texas.[2]

In 1862 Abraham Lincoln signed the Morrill Act, which provided federal funding for the establishment of a land-grant college in every state in the Union—including, after the war, those in the economically devastated South. The postwar political climate in Alabama, however, delayed the establishment of Alabama's land-grant institution until 1872.

Donation of the East Alabama Male College buildings and land most likely tipped the scales in Auburn's favor in a fight with the University of Alabama and other locations over placement of the new Alabama college. The delay between acceptance of the Morrill Act provisions in 1867 and the legislative authorization for the school in 1872 left time for a long and bitter struggle.[3]

The fight between the University of Alabama and Auburn over territory and funding began in 1867 and has continued into recent years, but the fight over racial discrimination inherent in the "separate but equal" system of education set up in postwar Alabama was postponed until 1964. In 1875 the Alabama legislature approved bills that established four "normal" schools for whites and four for blacks, and the Colored Normal School at Huntsville became Alabama Agricultural and Mechanical College. When President Lyndon B. Johnson signed the Civil Rights Act of 1964, the "dual Extension system came crashing down" and there were "drastic changes that had to be made in agricultural programs supported by federal funds." It took the 1969 *Strain v. Philpott* class-action suit, however, to make it happen.[4] In 1872 the ideals inherent in the Morrill Act did, however, address the problem of class discrimination in the state of Alabama.

Higher education had been strictly traditional and classical, designed for the training of doctors, lawyers, preachers, and teachers. The Morrill Act sought a kind of education of college grade that would be suitable for the man on the farm and the man in the workshop and which would make their work more effective. It proposed to dignify the many walks of life with knowledge and efficiency, to open the door of educational opportunity to all.[5]

In his book *Colleges for Our Land and Time*, Edward Danforth Eddy Jr. identified "a clear and unique pattern, sometimes termed a trilogy of American ingenuity," in the characteristics common to land-grant institutions. These are "instruction, research, and extension," and they mark a change in the educational pattern of higher education "most vividly" "in their prevailing social consciousness."[6]

In 1872, however, women as well as African Americans were denied admittance to the land-grant college at Auburn. Women would gain access to the advantages of the institution during the administration of Auburn's fourth president, William LeRoy Broun, a "brilliant graduate of the University of Virginia in 1850" who served as "commandant of the Confederate Arsenal at Richmond during the Civil War." Broun's tenure at Auburn (1882–83 and 1884–1902) was interrupted when he "failed to win acceptance of proposed curriculum changes in favor of scientific education," and Broun resigned after his first year. His replacement, David Boyd, "won acceptance of Broun's recommendations" and returned to Louisiana State University. Broun returned to Auburn and "completely remade the basic courses of study. . . . With the aid of a state tax on fertilizer, levied in 1883, and the passage of the Federal Hatch Act of 1887, Dr. Broun was able to acquire land for an Experiment Station and prepare the college for a thorough system of agricultural research."[7]

The laboratory method was expensive, but the reluctant board accepted it when they rehired Broun in 1884. President Broun believed that Auburn's educational mission was greater than that of an agricultural and mechanical college. Auburn historians Joe Yeager and Gene Stevenson recognized Broun's leadership: "President Broun's philosophy and intellect were ideally suited for leading Alabama's Land-Grant College toward its destiny as an institution of technical education in all its fields of study, including agriculture." In 1902, Auburn's sixth president, Charles C. Thach, called Broun a "forerunner" who established at Auburn "several scientific departments hitherto unattempted in the South. One of those . . . was a 'first-class biological laboratory,' which set in place an emphasis on the biological sciences that continues to define Auburn University."[8]

In 1892 Broun succeeded in convincing the Board of Trustees to admit women to the college. Many at Auburn, including Broun's own daughter, Kate, had been at the forefront of the movement for coeducational higher education. Members of the faculty and their wives, especially Annie White Mell, had argued for years for the admittance of women. President Broun's success with the board made the land-grant college at Auburn "the first university in the state to allow women to matriculate."[9] Broun's daughter and two friends were admitted in 1892, and "at the commencement exercises in 1894, Alabama Governor Thomas Goode Jones escorted each coed to the rostrum to receive her degree 'amid thunderous applause.'"[10]

In 1905, the third director of the Agricultural Experiment Station, John Frederick Duggar, who became world-famous for his pioneering cotton and legume experiments, was living in the old Darby farmhouse, and the prized bull of Alabama Polytechnic Institute (API) was occupying the barn located on the now oak-shaded lawn of the President's Home. In 1913 the first public sale of livestock at Auburn was held on the grounds where children play when Auburn University hosts its annual "Family Fun Day."

In 1912, Frances Camp Duggar, "A daughter of Auburn legend John F. Duggar," appeared "in that year's Glomerata and [was] called the 'first agricultural co-ed.'"[11] (In 2006, women graduates of the College of Veterinary Medicine outnumbered the men.)

A little further up the hill from the President's Home, the oldest continuous experiment in cotton crop rotation in the nation, begun by Duggar, is still engaged in experimental study. Just south of the house, on the grounds now designated for the Davis Arboretum, an experimental pond of carp provided facts for the first bulletin of the State Agricultural Experiment Station, dated October 10, 1883.[12]

In 1937 the Duggar/Darby farmhouse burned and made the site of the President's Home available for the residence of President Luther N. Duncan. From a farm in northwest Alabama, Duncan had come to the Agricultural and Mechanical College in 1896 and graduated from API in 1900. He admired the determined ideals of President Broun, who persuaded the board to change the name of the college from Alabama A&M to Alabama Polytechnic Institute, saying at the board meeting of January 13, 1897, that the "college has entered a larger sphere to teach science and its application as related to the varied industrial interests of civilization."[13]

In 1902, Broun died at the age of seventy-four "while dressing to go to the office. At that time, Auburn had nineteen professors and ten assistants, 403 male students and nine coeds." Broun's "greatest genius," according to tenth Auburn president Ralph Draughon, "lay in his ability to select and bring to the faculty a remarkable group of young men, many of whom were destined to shape the institution and guide it for fifty years after his death."[14]

Although the President's Home at Auburn is set on the corner of College Street and Samford Avenue, the house itself faces Mell Street, named for Patrick H. Mell, who came to the Agricultural and Mechanical College in 1878 from his position as state chemist of Georgia to serve as professor of natural history and modern languages. In addition to teaching geology, mineralogy, meteorology, botany, zoology, entomology, natural philosophy, telegraphy, civil engineering, mining engineering, and French, Mell established a museum of fossils and minerals that included zoological and botanical specimens. He founded the Alabama Weather Service and invented a system of weather signal flags that was adopted by the National Weather Service. He also served as the second director of the Agriculture Experiment Station.[15] Mell and many other outstanding teachers who served the college under President Broun raised the noble purpose of the Morrill Act to legendary status.

The name of the college at Auburn had been changed to Auburn University when the Civil Rights Act of 1964 opened the opportunities of the land-grant institution at Auburn to African Americans. During the tenure of the school's tenth president, Ralph Draughon, graduate student Harold Franklin was briefly enrolled in the university, but his admittance was enough to open the doors to others. Franklin was not, however, the first black man to be associated with the mission of the land-grant college. In 1906, Tom Campbell of Tuskegee had become the first black county agent in the nation, and when the Smith-Lever Act of 1915 made the farm extension work of the U.S. Department of Agriculture a state-federal partnership, many of the agents operating in Tuskegee "came under the administrative leadership of Auburn's renowned J. F. Duggar."[16]

When President Duncan selected the setting for the President's Home in 1939, he built his official residence at the southern entrance to the API campus on US Highway 29 (College Street) and set the home's porch facing a massive and much-needed campus rebuild-

President Luther Duncan (1935–47) proclaims a "Greater Auburn Day" in 1939. (Auburn University Special Collections)

ing campaign funded by Franklin Delano Roosevelt's Public Works Administration. From that porch, Dr. Duncan might have watched the completion of the first four dorms for women, generally referred to as "The Quad." Duncan also built the first tiny part of what is now Jordan-Hare Stadium, but the stadium was probably not visible from the porch of the President's Home at that time.

To celebrate the major achievement of his building campaign, Duncan promoted the "Greater Auburn Day" event, attended by three thousand people, which was held on the Auburn campus in 1939. For this, an ill Luther Duncan climbed the stairs to Samford Tower and rang the old bell that had been silent for several years.

The size of the campus at Auburn tripled during Duncan's administration. FDR and later his wife Eleanor came to visit the campus. The young wife of Auburn's eloquent history teacher and tenth president, Ralph Draughon, remembered that Roosevelt had come to review the military cadet corps: "Everyone in the county turned out to see him, even the small children and their nurses, waving to him as they sat in front of the KA House. Dr. and Mrs. Duncan, Ralph and I with all of the trustees and college military officials waited in the

Auburn welcomes FDR to the campus of Alabama Polytechnic Institute, spring 1939. (Auburn University Special Collections)

View from the faculty cottages to the President's Home, early 1940s. (Auburn University Photographic Services)

President Ralph B. Draughon (1948–65) dedicates the Garden of Memory on June 5, 1954. (Auburn University Special Collections)

reviewing stand which was back of where the quad dining hall now stands overlooking the drill field. Finally, here came the car bearing the President accompanied by Senator Lister Hill and Representative Henry Steagall, Sr. . . . [there was] much flag waving and cheers."[17]

Standing on the hill of the President's Home in 1941, Dr. Duncan would have had a panoramic view of a campus that had begun to change dramatically. During and after World War II, the campus exploded with students, and housing for GIs and their families began to crowd the vista of traditional coeducational dorms and overrun the open spaces with all manner of makeshift living quarters.

On June 5, 1954, the campus perspective from the President's Home was altered in honor of the many men and women of API who had served the nation during World War I, World War II, and the Korean conflict. A Garden of Memory was established by the Alabama Federation of Garden Clubs, in partnership with API, just across Mell Street in front of the President's Home. It is appropriate that this memorial to Auburn's war effort was dedicated by President Draughon.

While serving the college under Dr. Duncan, Ralph Draughon had endeared himself to the town and to the college with his "Christmas Letter to the Boys, 1943." Draughon sent news to the battlefront from "the Auburn Family." He recalled the glorious 1942 football season and remembered the team's outstanding players. Life in Auburn was different without the boys, Draughon said, "but no college in the country is making a finer contribution to the Nation."[18]

Throughout the history of the college at Auburn, military science had been a part of the required curriculum for all cadets (this ended with the end of the draft after the Vietnam War). Military training had been the key to passage of the Morrill Act in 1862, and during World War II the Army Specialized Training Program and the Engineering Science, Management and War Training Program at API enrolled 38,506 persons.[19]

With an emphasis on land-grant ideals—that is, a focus on the principles of scientific inquiry and a dedication to the mission of service—Auburn, first as Alabama Agricultural and Mechanical College and then as Alabama Polytechnic Institute, became a great asset to the people of the state and the nation. However, the increasing enrollment in the liberal-arts curriculum after World War II counterbalanced API's primarily agricultural identity and brought the emphasis of a liberal education at Auburn full-circle. In 1960, during the Draughon administration, the college at Auburn reached the pinnacle of its identity as Auburn University.

On College Street just south of the President's Home in the middle of the Cullars Rotation (the oldest soil fertility experiment in the South and the second-oldest continuous cotton experiment in the world) the Jule Collins Smith Museum of Art was built in 2003. Beyond the President's Home and the museum on College Street, the new Auburn University Research Park was begun in 2007. Auburn's seventeenth president, Ed Richardson, believes the park will be essential to the changing mission of Auburn University.

In 2006, the view of the campus from the President's Home had changed significantly from the time that Ralph Draughon Jr. gazed across the campus as a child in the 1950s: "All sorts of buildings and developments today have obstructed the view from the portico of the president's home, but when I first knew the house only fields and pastures stretched out for miles to the west towards the Wire Road and beyond. I remember vividly the spectacular sunsets that were then a special feature of the prospect from the front terrace. They made me realize on what a fine site the house stands."[20]

CHAPTER TWO

The Home

The front page of the 1938 Christmas issue of the *Auburn Alumnus* (now *Auburn Magazine*) showed President Luther N. Duncan breaking ground for the President's Home at Alabama Polytechnic Institute. An article within the alumni magazine offered details of the project: "The President's Home was the first WPA project started and work began November 24, 1938. This building was designed by Warren, Knight and Davis, Birmingham, Alabama, and was built by Brice Building Company, Birmingham, Alabama, for $38,412.00."[1]

The President's Home is an extension of the president's office at Samford Hall. It is the place provided for the president of Auburn University to continue to meet the social requirements of his office

On the site of the Agricultural Experiment director's home, President Luther Duncan sets a home place for Auburn's presidents, November 1938. (Auburn University Special Collections)

in an after-hours setting. In her notes on life in the President's Home, Mrs. Caroline Draughon cataloged the types of entertaining required of the Auburn president and First Lady: "Parties for the trustees, town and gown, alumni and their wives, politicians, business executives, faculty, students."[2]

When Dr. and Mrs. Duncan occupied the President's Home at Auburn, Ralph Draughon Jr. was playmate to the Duncan's only grandson, Robert. In 2006, Ralph remembered the boyhood games he and Robert played there in the 1940s.

> I first visited the house as a little boy in the early days of the Second World War when Bob Duncan . . . and I built a fort under the dining room table to defend the house from invasion by the Axis powers. Incidentally, it was the longest dining room table I had ever seen. I remember Mrs. Duncan, who was the most affectionate and indulgent of grandmothers, leaning down with some amusement to check on us from time to time. Bob was commanding officer, I definitely served as his subordinate, and Pork, the butler at the time, was drafted not very willingly as the supply sergeant and required from time to time to bring us rations from the kitchen.[3]

Before the Draughons moved into the President's Home in 1948, the official purpose of the home and the warmth of its family life were missing. Ralph recalled that the courtyard had become a place for student rendezvous:

> After Dr. Duncan's death, when my father served as acting president for more than a year, the house stood empty, and the driveway became a very convenient lover's lane for the students. One couple first got "pinned" in the driveway and then later on they got engaged there. One of the first issues my father had to deal with when the trustees finally chose him president was this same couple's request to get married on the front lawn. Buildings and Grounds department wasn't very enthusiastic about the project, and my father thought

Students in front of the President's Home at Alabama Polytechnic Institute, early 1940s. (Auburn University Special Collections)

President Harry Philpott (1965–80) and his family in front of the official residence at Auburn University, May 1966. (Auburn University Photographic Services)

> it would be a very bad precedent. Besides, he asked, "what will that couple want to do next out there?"[4]

During the sixteen-year residence of the Draughon family, the President's Home was open to thousands of official guests and numerous friends, family, and students. Mrs. Harry Philpott, who raised her four children in the President's Home, stated emphatically: "This is the children's home too. It is a home for all six Philpotts—not just a 'state home.'"[5]

Throughout its existence, the President's Home at Auburn University has known the children and grandchildren of nine official families. The grandchildren of the Richardson family have spun around the grounds in go-carts and competed with their parents in croquet tournaments on the lawn. From forts under the dining room table to tents set up in the sunroom, from teasing their siblings on the back porch to meeting their dates at the door, the children and grandchildren of the President's Home have left the place with lots of memories.

The President's Home had been standing for more than fifty years when R. G. Millman described it in his 1991 booklet, *The Auburn University Walking Tour Guide.* The Martin family was occupying the home at the time, and in a chapter titled "The Windshield Tour," Millman described the "six stately wooden columns supporting the porch roof that extends across the entire front of the two-story central block."[6] These columns looked the same in 2006 in spite of the sparks that raced up one of them in 1994 when a painter tried to remove old paint with a torch.

In 1991 a look inside the central block of the house revealed a double foyer extending from front to back with a grand staircase at the back and a door opening onto a screened porch. This was true in 2006, but when the Philpott family moved into the home in 1965 the screened porch became a family room.

Guests who came to the President's Home were greeted at the palatial front door and flowed through the foyer to the back porch before returning to the dining room on the left of the foyer for dinner. The living room is on the right when one enters the home, and it extends from the front of the house to the back.

In the foyer of the President's Home, Mrs. Richardson with Kammi and Jon Waggoner, executive council, and Brian Keeter, executive liaison, fall 2006. (Auburn University Photographic Services)

Between the two double-hung windows at the front of the living room, the American mahogany secretary seems perfectly placed. It was an official gift to President Duncan from the estate of Alabama Governor Charles Henderson. The piece is a nineteenth-century reproduction. The grandfather clock in the foyer was also part of the Henderson gift and had to be brought to Auburn in an unconventional way (some say a hearse was used; others think Dr. Duncan might have sent for the clock in a vintage military vehicle). The Westminster chimes of the clock (a German-style mahogany reproduction made in Grand Rapids, Michigan, in the same period as the secretary) resounded so loudly that the clock stands silent now in its place in the foyer beside the grand staircase.

The formal dining room and informal breakfast room of the President's Home have seen scrumptious dinners served to scores

Interior views of the President's Home. (Photos: Auburn University Photographic Services)

of official guests, family, and friends who have sat at the tables or stood in the buffet line. Over the years, lots of steaming pots of tea and coffee have been poured beside antique silver trays laden with delicious desserts.

Beyond the living room, the sunroom also extends the width of the house and opens onto the formal garden through double, glass-paned doors. This room has served several unique purposes. It has been the official gathering place for guests dining to the music of the grand piano, and it has witnessed momentous events like the contract signing of Ralph "Shug" Jordan and the lying in state of President Duncan. The 1947 *Auburn Alumnus Special Memorial Edition* described the earliest of these events: "From 10 a.m. this morning until shortly before funeral services at 5 p.m. . . . the body of Auburn's beloved president lay in state in the beautiful, flower-banked south parlor of the president's home. . . . There high on a hill over looking the greater Auburn which his life-long efforts had built, a military guard stood by his casket."[7]

President Luther Duncan lying in state in the official residence in 1947—a scene most unlikely for any university president today. (Auburn University Special Collections)

When the Draughon family came to the President's Home, they brought their personal cook and friend to prepare the family meals and assist Mrs. Draughon with official entertaining. Ruth Dallas was there on family occasions too, like the wedding reception of the Draughon's only daughter, Ann. Ann's brother remembered the event:

> My sister later was married from the house (in the Episcopal Church downtown), but the reception was held at the home. No alcoholic beverages were served downstairs [Lee County Alabama was "dry" at the time], but my father had decreed that a bar would be set up in an upstairs guest room, mostly for his older male friends. My assignment was to go through the crowd and direct his friends to the bar. I was supposed to be discreet, but "Miss Molly" Hollifield Jones, a social leader of rather imposing appearance, overheard me. She created quite a stir in the crowd by demanding to know in stentorian tones (but in fun) where a bar had been set up for the *ladies* who were attending the reception.[8]

Legendary coach Ralph "Shug" Jordan signs his contract, January 1951. (Auburn University Photographic Services)

In the breakfast room of the President's Home, family butler and cook, Jim Smith and Ruth Dallas, with Ann Draughon on her wedding day in 1956. (Auburn University Special Collections)

When the Philpotts lived in the President's Home, Dr. and Mrs. Philpott both pitched in to prepare the food for official guests as well as for their own large family.

In the 2006 kitchen, which was completely remodeled after the fire of 1994, there are new cabinets, granite countertops, and a white-tiled backsplash with various hand-painted and hand-labeled wildflowers. This artistic touch was added by local artist Montaign Mathison, wife of the minister of the Auburn Methodist Church. Several of Mrs. Mathison's oils were also purchased for the President's Home when the Muses lived in the house (1992–2001).

From the kitchen there is a small stairwell that is used by the family to go up to the bedrooms and by the staff to access the basement, where the bar setups and other things for events are stored. Next to these stairs is a small den that has been used through the years as a private place for the president's family.

The "five gabled dormers behind a balustrade [on the second-floor roof of the President's Home] and chimneys at each end . . . flanked with quarter-round lights" are described in Millman's

(Top left) President and Mrs. Martin (1984–92) receive the press in the sunroom after Dr. Martin's selection as Auburn's fourteenth president, spring 1984. (Auburn University Special Collections)

(Bottom right) A Richardson family gathering, Thanksgiving 2006. (Auburn University Photographic Services)

Wearing an apron given to him when he was dean of religion at Stevens College, Dr. Philpott whips up delicious desserts. (Auburn University Special Collections)

President Harry Philpott, in his official capacity as ordained Baptist minister, watches his daughter approach the altar on the arm of her older brother, Mel. (Courtesy of Jeanne P. Bankester)

"Windshield Tour."[9] But the chimney at the kitchen end of the house exists only to provide symmetry for the structure; there is no fireplace there. The home's only fireplace is between the living room and the large sunroom. Set in the chimney of this fireplace on the upper-floor level is a small window that provides light for the bathroom between the upstairs bedrooms. It also offers a bird's-eye view of the formal garden, which was captured by a wedding photographer on one of its loveliest days.

In the formal garden is a small rectangular building that resembles a Roman bathhouse. It has a red tile floor and a blue tile backsplash with a lion's-head waterspout set over a small basin. Nothing about the design and construction of this little building could be found in 2006, although an article in the *Auburn Plainsman* of October 1940 described the formal garden and its "bathhouse" as "only about half fin-

In the formal garden, President and Mrs. Ralph Draughon receive guests and members of the Board of Trustees, which included Governor "Big Jim" Folsom, ex officio president of the API board, fall 1949. (Auburn University Special Collections)

ished." By December of that year, however, the *Plainsman* was describing the landscaping of the President's Home as "practically completed" and "designed for the graceful handling of the many large official and social functions which the President is called upon to give."[10]

When the Richardson family came to live in the President's Home, the pool at the end of the garden was cleaned and repaired. The Richardsons kept the fountains in the garden and in the parking area pool in front of the house spouting every day. At Christmastime in 2005, a tree shaped by tiny orange lights was set over the fountain in the garden pool, and a larger tree of blue lights was placed over the fountain in the larger pool in front of the President's Home.

In the early spring of 2006 a tour of the formal garden of the President's Home was part of the first "Art in Bloom" event to promote the Jule Collins Smith Museum of Art, and Mrs. Richardson discovered that the two garden statues, both depicting a young goddess pouring from pitcher to cup, are classical and neoclassical variations of Hebes, Greek goddess of women and youth.

The President's Home and its gardens have been enjoyed by many visitors and official guests. The house and grounds have been loved and tended by the families of the nine Auburn University presidents and First Ladies who have made the house a home since 1939.

Christmas fountain, 2005.
(Auburn University
Photographic Services)

Neoclassical Hebes in the garden of the President's Home. (Auburn University Photographic Services)

Classical Hebes in the garden of the President's Home. (Auburn University Photographic Services)

"Art in Bloom" flora and fauna lecture at the President's Home, February 2006. (Auburn University Photographic Services)

"Family Fun Day" on the front lawn of the President's Home, spring 2004. (Auburn University Photographic Services)

CHAPTER THREE

The Duncans

1935–1947

Luther Noble and Annie Smith Duncan were the first family to live in the new President's Home on the edge of the Auburn campus. In 1939, Dr. Duncan had been president of Alabama Polytechnic Institute for more than four years. Luther and Annie Duncan met in Wetumpka in 1900 when they were both teachers at the high school there. He directed the agriculture classes, and she taught elocution. Five years after his graduation from API, Luther Duncan had returned to Auburn with his wife and two young daughters, Mary Elizabeth and Margaret Susan. The Duncans' only son, Robert, was born in Auburn.

In 1875 Luther Duncan was born on a farm in Franklin County near Russellville that his granddaughter describes as very modest and "out in the middle of nowhere." In 1896, Luther came to college at Auburn and lived with his older brother, George, and sister-in-law, Julia. George was principal of Auburn Grammar School, and according to Edith Judd, wife of the college's dean of education, Julia "held every position of leadership that Auburn could offer" and was "a strong influence in every life that touched hers." As a student at Alabama Agricultural and Mechanical College, Luther Duncan was president of his class. In 1900, during the tenure of President LeRoy Broun, Duncan graduated from Alabama Polytechnic Institute with highest honors.

Annie Smith was born in Livingston, Alabama, in 1879 and graduated from Livingston Normal School under Julia Tutwiler. On becoming the ninth president of the college at Auburn, Dr. Duncan gave credit to his wife, his mother, and his sister-in-law for his success.[1]

Luther Duncan began his career at API in 1905 as an instructor of agriculture. In 1909, "in cooperation with the United States Department of Agriculture, an extension unit was created . . . in the College of Agricultural Sciences." This unit was called the Department of School Agriculture or Agricultural Extension Work, and Duncan headed the department.[2]

In 1920, after the death of President Charles C. Thach, Governor Thomas E. Kilby appointed the state superintendent of education, Spright Dowell, president of API, and Dowell chose Duncan as the first full-time director of the Alabama Cooperative Extension Service. On the campus of API, Duncan organized the Alabama Farm Bureau (the state branch of the American Farm Bureau), which provided cooperative purchasing and marketing for Alabama farmers.

In the 1920s, the power of the Alabama Cooperative Extension Service spread throughout the state and dominated the development of API. County agents connected to the Extension Service in Auburn were well known and generally well respected within the counties they served. In addition to their service to the farmers and farm families of Alabama, these men and women recruited students for API, and helped foster the reputation of the college throughout the state. Auburn was respected as a place of higher education in practical subjects that could help ordinary people, especially farmers, improve their lives. Via the extension agents of Auburn and owing to the farm families of Alabama, API became a politically powerful institution during the Duncan administration. In 1942, gubernatorial candidate James E. "Big Jim" Folsom, who was very popular with the people of Alabama, solicited the support of Luther Duncan and the Extension Service. He did not receive it, however, and Folsom would later accuse Duncan of using the power of the Extension Service to defeat him.

During the Great Depression, the amount of federal money going into Duncan's organization in comparison to the lack of money available to President Knapp for paying the faculty and running the college caused a fight between the president and the Extension director. When Knapp resigned, many people wanted Duncan to be appointed president, but Governor Benjamin M. Miller recommended that a committee of three (Duncan and Deans John Wilmore and Bolling Crenshaw) be formed to administer API until a new president could be selected. Duncan's hard work and leadership in this group as well as the reelection of his friend Governor Bibb Graves paid off, and in 1935 Dr. Luther Duncan took charge as president of API. His appointment was announced at the state capital in Montgomery on February 22, 1935. On his return to Auburn afterwards, Dr. Duncan and his wife greeted members of the town and gown in front of the former president's home (now Katherine Cater Hall). The event was reported in the *Auburn Alumnus* by Edith Judd, who said that the town siren was sounded at seven o'clock that evening and "a great concourse of people, led by the Mayor, flocked to the Mansion where President and Mrs. Duncan received them in front of their future home." There Dr. Duncan made a speech honoring President Broun and others he had known in his student days: "From these great teachers I caught the spirit of Auburn, which to me is the spirit of growth and progress; the spirit of helpfulness and service; the spirit of equality of opportunity, which is real democracy."[3]

When he became president, Duncan stated that due to the economic hardships of the past three years at Auburn, "our faculty has earned $515,238.80 which it did not and perhaps never will receive."[4] Auburn was placed on probation by the Southern Association of Colleges and Schools "until full salaries were resumed for faculty members and per-student expenditures were increased." Auburn was more than a million dollars in debt, and the faculty was suffering when Duncan became president, but he "rallied political support in the state and exploited every possible financial program of the New Deal." In competition with the University of Alabama for state funding, "Duncan used agriculture people and the University of Alabama's president used lawyers as their power blocks."[5]

Mrs. Duncan's family heritage had been established in colonial America, and she was extremely proud of her lifelong membership in the Daughters of the American Revolution and other organizations such as the Auburn Woman's Club. When her husband became director of the Extension Service, Mrs. Duncan's social engagements increased. From the 1920s through the 1940s, numerous teas and receptions hosted by Mrs. Duncan can be found on the social pages of all the Auburn newspapers, including the *Auburn Plainsman.*

According to her only granddaughter, Ann Pearson, Mrs. Duncan was also a practical woman who "loved to hook rugs, and was very good at it." In conversation with the author, Ann said that she still had "several of [her grandmother's] best efforts" at Noble Hall, an antebellum mansion Dr. Duncan bought in the 1940s. Over the years Mrs. Duncan became "a rather good amateur artist," Ann said, and one of Mrs. Duncan's still lifes of magnolias was still hanging in the parlor of the Woman's Club in 2006.

That Mrs. Duncan found time to pursue her arts and crafts during the twelve years she served Auburn as First Lady is remarkable. She seems to have been continually giving or attending teas where the use of anything other than fine china and sterling silver would have been socially unacceptable. As with her insistence on being able to use language properly, Mrs. Duncan remained loyal to the social requirements of her day, even in her Christmas gifts to Ann. In an article she wrote for the *Auburn Bulletin,* Ann said that "at the time of my birth [my grandmother] picked out a silver pattern for me—Chantilly, a good, solid never-out-of-stock design and just the thing for a girl's hope chest. And every Christmas (and birthday) I got another piece."[6]

Dr. and Mrs. Duncan seemed to have been perfectly matched in their belief that one should strive to present oneself well in every situation. As director of the Extension Service, Duncan believed that a good extension agent should be "mature" and "have unbounded energy, zeal, optimism, enthusiasm and persistency [*sic*]. He must have habits which come only from the very highest character."[7]

Mrs. Duncan's job-training skills were remembered well by Ralph Draughon Jr.: "Luckily for Auburn University, its president's home had for several decades a butler, Jim Smith, who impressed all visitors with his courtesy, his demeanor, and his bearing. Butlers currently are in short supply, and I'm sure that no billionaire today has a butler to compare with Jim. . . . In one of her many important contributions to life in the president's home, Mrs. Duncan had trained him, very ably, and he turned out to be an apt pupil. If memory serves me, she preferred to call him James, but the Draughons all called him Jim because, I suppose, we were too fond of him to be formal."[8]

Speaking of her grandmother's expectations for her, Ann Pearson remembered the many nights that Mrs. Duncan would insist that her granddaughter strive to master orally the literary works of Sir Walter Scott: "I think she was especially fond of him because he inevitably, and eternally, rhymed off. She broke me in on the delicacies of oral delivery with *The Lady of the Lake*, and she encouraged me to commit long passages to memory and recite them."[9]

In 1942, when their son, Lt. Robert Duncan, was called to active duty, the Duncans hosted "a large group of friends" at a farewell dinner that included Robert's grandmother, Susan Smith, who had come to live at the President's Home in the 1940s.[10]

Dr. Luther N. Duncan died in office, as had his mentor, President Wm. LeRoy Broun. Dr. B. F. Thomas Sr., a physician known and loved by generations of Auburn people, told officials that Dr. Duncan had been taken to Drake Infirmary on the morning of July 26, 1947, where he had died of a heart attack.[11] Ann Pearson was only six years old when her grandfather died, but she remembered that he had enjoyed quail hunting and pitching horseshoes. He also taught her how to fish.

At the meeting held by the Council of Deans after Duncan's death, the dean of agriculture, Marion Funchess, recalled the words Duncan had expressed in 1939 regarding Auburn's mission: "The great problem of Alabama is that of low income of her people, and lower incomes are found among the farm families of the state. . . . To this end, all the efforts of the Alabama Polytechnic Institute through teaching, extension, and research . . . are bent toward improving farm life through better farm practices, conservation of soil, and conservation of human lives."[12]

Luther Duncan was a dynamic president who was determined to bring the institution he had loved since 1896 into a prominence so permanent that no one could deny its significance or its contribution to education in Alabama and in the nation. Before the end of his life, Duncan would see the value of Auburn's research in many areas that improved the lives of farmers and expanded the Alabama economy significantly.

Although he could not see it from the porch of the President's Home, President Duncan thought that the most beautiful spot on the Auburn campus was found at the Bibb Graves Amphitheater, which he had also constructed and where "more than 2000 people gathered to pay respects to the late president."[13]

Mrs. Duncan died on October 14, 1951, her husband's birthday, and both are buried in Auburn's historic Pine Hill Cemetery.

Annie Smith Duncan, teacher of elocution, social lady of "town and gown," and wife of the politically astute ninth president of the institution that would become Auburn University, circa 1900. (Courtesy of Ann Pearson)

This photograph is found in the antebellum home Dr. Duncan bought his family in the early 1940s. (Courtesy of Ann Pearson)

The First Lady of Auburn hooking rugs in the President's Home, 1940s. (Courtesy of Ann Pearson)

On the campus of Alabama Polytechnic Institute, students of the war years greet Dr. Duncan. (Auburn University Special Collections)

On the parking court in front of the President's Home, Dr. Duncan supports the students of Alabama Polytechnic Institute in an old southern tradition, early 1940s. (Auburn University Special Collections)

President Duncan speaks informally in the sunroom of the President's Home, 1940s. (Auburn University Special Collections)

On the steps of the President's Home, Dr. and Mrs. Duncan send their son, Robert, to the war, 1942. (Courtesy of Ann Pearson)

CHAPTER FOUR

The Draughons

1947–1965

Ralph Draughon was born in Hartford, Alabama, in 1900 and graduated from Alabama Polytechnic Institute in 1922. He taught history before becoming principal of the new high school in Orrville, Alabama, the hometown of his future wife, Caroline Marshall. The future First Lady of Auburn was a popular teenager at the time, ten years younger than Ralph and attending high school in nearby Selma. In the summer of 1929, however, Ralph and Caroline were both students at API. Ralph was pursuing a graduate degree in history, and Caroline was taking classes she could apply to her undergraduate degree at the Women's College of Alabama (now Huntingdon College in Montgomery).

The Draughons married in Orrville after Caroline's graduation in 1931, and the newlyweds rented an upstairs apartment in the Lawson house (now called Greystone) in Auburn. George Petrie, API's renowned dean of history, had offered his former student, Ralph, a temporary teaching position in the history department. Caroline's brother Albert and Ralph's brother James lived with the young couple so that the boys could attend API. Ralph's teaching position became permanent upon the unexpected death of Professor W. P. Brown.[1]

Like most of the API faculty during the Great Depression, the Draughons often went without pay or with only a partial salary, and were forced to live on credit for their groceries and medicine. When Ralph became secretary to the Board of Trustees and academic assistant to President Duncan, things changed for the Draughons. The economic depression that had gripped the nation was easing, and President Duncan had begun to erase the college's debts and increase faculty salaries.

After World War II, Ralph Draughon was responsible for rebuilding the college faculty and providing housing and educational opportunities for the thousands of students who came to the college. As historian Martin Olliff writes, "The GI Bill had inundated API with students—doubling enrollment twice between 1944 and 1948. API's physical plant and faculty were too small to handle the onslaught effectively. Throughout his tenure, Draughon worked with state and federal officials to get building and operating funds to improve campus facilities and its faculty."[2]

In *Caroline Marshall Draughon,* Auburn historian Leah Rawls Atkins details the life of the young faculty wife in 1940s Auburn: "She served as room mother at her children's schools. She poured tea at college functions, attended meetings of the United Daughters of the Confederacy, PEO [an exclusive organization for women associated with higher education] and the [Auburn] Woman's Club, played bridge, or joined her sewing club for lunch. She was active in the Episcopal Church Women and the Altar Guild."[3]

When President Duncan died in 1947, Ralph was appointed acting president of API, and Ralph and Caroline were obliged to become personally involved in the trustees' search for a new president. The trustees were then perhaps interviewing candidates with executive experience at major colleges, universities, or corporations, as well as persons of high rank in the military or government services. In her notes, Mrs. Draughon recalls the experience: "I entertained many candidates of this caliber in my small home, using my own silver and china, etc., but with the help of my faithful cook and friend, Ruth Dallas. . . . The business office allowed me $2.50 for each guest, a far cry from what is permitted today, I'm sure!"[4]

Although that search resulted in the selection of an Auburn man, as has often been the case at Auburn, the Draughons were surprised when Governor James E. "Big Jim" Folsom, ex officio president of the API Board of Trustees, announced the board's decision in October 1948.

Ralph Brown Draughon, tenth president at Auburn, was inaugurated on May 12, 1949, in Cliff Hare Stadium with "colorful" ceremonies and a "host of guests," according to the *Auburn Plainsman.*[5] On being selected president, Ralph had said that the job was a big one for a fisherman; and the *Auburn Alumnews* of October 1948 said Caroline enjoyed gardening, flower arranging, cooking, entertaining, and caring for her children as well as fishing with her husband. Caroline was described as the supportive wife who "sews well, cooks well, and can even dress a string of fish caught by her fisherman husband."[6]

In 1948 Caroline was "given permission to redecorate the President's home," and in 1985 she spoke of that responsibility: "With assistance from Jack Simms' sister, Millie, [and others] . . . We did a very creditable job, I thought." They chose rattan furniture and a "grasscloth" carpet, popular items in the 1950s. Many of these furnishings remained in the sunroom of the President's Home for more than forty years.

In her notes on life in the President's Home, Mrs. Draughon recalled: "An ecstatic Jim Smith was returned to the home as butler and chauffeur, and what wonderful help he was! . . . He *loved* his job, and asked permission to wear white gloves when he served dinner for guests, but I assured him we had not reached that status."[7]

Jim Smith also assisted Mrs. Draughon in many other ways, as Ralph Draughon Jr. remembers well: "Jim had many duties, including 'Hoovering' the downstairs with a vacuum cleaner and serving as the college chauffeur. Furthermore, when I arrived at my teenage years, my parents, probably in desperation, put Jim in charge of me. One of his duties was to get me up in the morning so I could go to school. It was, I'm embarrassed to recall, not an easy task. On most school days, it took him at least two trips upstairs. On the first trip, he would make me get out of bed, and on the second trip he would wake me up where I had gone to sleep on the floor."[8]

The Draughons' popular daughter, Ann, was unhappy about living in the President's Home and entertaining her friends there. The official entertaining required of the president's family added to her dismay. According to her brother, Ralph, Ann's first experience with hosting the state's governor was shocking:

> She felt some alarm in one early incident at the house, when my parents honored the new Governor of Alabama, "Big Jim" Folsom, with a reception in the formal garden. People today probably don't realize what a sensation "Big Jim" created when he first arrived on the political scene. He seemed larger than life. . . . For the reception in his honor he showed up early, but while the last minute preparations for the event were being made, he disappeared. Nobody was sure where he had gone, and my sixteen-year-old sister was dispatched to find him. She finally traced him to an upstairs guest room, and when she knocked very timidly on the door, the Governor called out, "Hey there, honey! Come on in!" . . . She was really scared but delivered her message and fled.[9]

Ann Draughon had been a popular high school cheerleader, and her popularity continued during her student days at API. She was among the campus beauties selected by Powers and Associates in 1951.

"Miss Caroline" Draughon became tirelessly involved in numerous activities for the traditional students of Auburn, but she also saw the need to include activities for Auburn's surge of nontraditional students. She had taken up the duties of the president's wife honorably before her husband was officially president. She formed a new group called the Campus Club "to promote friendship and sociability among the women of various groups on the campus."[10]

Caroline also organized the Dames Club, wanting to involve the young wives who had taken secretarial jobs at the college in order to "put their husbands through school." Upon the graduation of her spouse, each member of the club would receive a PHT (Pushing Hubby Through) Certificate at a special ceremony. This "diploma" praised the wife's "willingness to make 'home' in a few small rooms, to wear old hose and pretend there were no runs; to spend late hours typing Hubby's thesis instead of dancing under the stars." The wives were praised as "the light of his life when he has needed you to shine the brightest."[11]

On the lawn of the President's Home every Easter, Mrs. Draughon hosted an egg hunt for the children of Dames Club members and other students. In 1965 the complex of apartments built in the 1950s for married students was named the Caroline Draughon Village in honor of Mrs. Draughon by the Auburn Board of Trustees. From 1965 to 2005 this complex, popularly known as the CDV, served the housing needs of thousands of married students.

One of the major accomplishments of Ralph Draughon's administration, as far as football fans are concerned, was the restoration of the football competition between Auburn and Alabama, which had ceased in 1907 due to a fight over the reimbursement requested by Auburn from Alabama for team expenses incurred in playing the 1907 game at Birmingham.[12] In 1948 Alabama became part of Auburn's fall football season, and in 1950 Auburn's legendary Coach Ralph Jordan was hired, much to the delight of Mrs. Draughon whose notes reflect this: "Ralph and Jeff Beard, the Athletic Director, set up a committee to hire a new coach. Many names were considered, but it all ended one Sunday afternoon with the committee meeting in my sunroom. No news reporters were allowed at the meeting, but they were all settled with me in the kitchen, butler's panty and garage. No two people were more excited over the selection of Coach 'Shug' Jordan than Bill [Beckwith] and I. 'Shug' and I had attended Selma High together and finished in the same class."[13]

Coach Jordan is remembered well for his Sunday-night television show of the 1950s and 1960s. For the press he "showed how it felt to be No. 1 in college football, hugging the Associated Press national championship trophy for his team, for his assistants, and for Auburn people everywhere. The Tigers hadn't had a winning season since 1942 when the former Auburn player and assistant coach took over the football program in 1951."[14]

During their years in the President's Home, Dr. and Mrs. Draughon were young enough to relate well to the students. These were the "happy days" of the 1950s, with popular television shows like *Ozzie and Harriet* and *Leave It to Beaver*. Caroline continued the practice of entertaining incoming freshmen by hosting a freshman picnic on the lawn of the President's Home every fall; and on her suggestion, the President's Reception (now a luncheon) was started and continues to be held for graduates and their parents before each graduation ceremony. The Draughons attended the fraternity dances and danced with the cadets at the spring Military Ball. Mrs. Draughon expressed fond memories of working with the legendary student deans of the 1950s and 1960s:

> While Dr. Duncan had been President, Ralph had the pleasure of interviewing and hiring young Katharine Cater as Dean of Women, and what a rare person she was! . . . as a first lady (and I never cared for that title) I found that Katharine Cater was most helpful in assisting me on the many social occasions for which I was responsible, especially the receptions for incoming freshmen, the four commencement parties per year, faculty receptions, and what one would term "town and gown" gatherings. (No cocktail parties in those days.) Katharine lived and had her office in what is now Cater Hall. I was always invited to receive with her at her annual spring and Christmas receptions when she entertained the senior women graduates, and the home mothers of the dormitories and the fraternities. These house mothers were carefully selected by her, and Dean Cater demanded that both women and men students adhere to all college rules. . . . Jim Foy, as Dean of men was equally as efficient in working with the men students.[15]

One of the housemothers hired during the Draughon administration was Lillian Carter, mother of U.S. President Jimmy Carter, who "served as Kappa Alpha housemother from 1956 through 1962."[16]

Martin Olliff states that Ralph Draughon "had a difficult relationship with the state's legislators" because of his emphasis on a "broad education" and his "control over the Extension Service."[17] In 1955, President Draughon suffered a heart attack that may have been brought on by the stress of his job. He recovered, however, and Mrs. Draughon notes the major project her husband wanted to accomplish before his retirement in 1965: "In the very late fifties, Ralph felt that our University needed an outstanding Library in order to be fully accredited. He asked Miss Kate Lane, Dr. Petrie's sister-in-law, and her wealthy niece in New York to donate the Petrie-Lane property for the building—and planned to name the Library after Dr. Petrie. The ladies refused and the college had to buy the property. My children and I are grateful that this building stands today as a memorial to a man . . . who really loved and struggled for this institution."[18]

In 1964 President and Mrs. Draughon experienced the most dramatic change to public education in the history of the state: the racial integration of the public schools and universities. Ralph Jr. remembered the stress that the changing times had placed upon his parents:

> In the era of massive resistance to racial integration in Alabama's public universities, the wives of college presidents suddenly found themselves on the front lines. The wife of the president of the University of Alabama was pelted with rotten eggs (and a picture of the incident appeared in Life Magazine) when [a student] unsuccessfully attempted to integrate the Tuscaloosa campus. Concerned for the safety of his wife as well as for the reputation of the college, my father began secret meetings with students and college officials very early on to prepare for the peaceful integration of Auburn. Since the president's home had been the focus of the riots at the University of Alabama, my father insisted that my mother attend the meetings, which were held in the sun room.[19]

In his summation of Ralph Draughon's tenure at Auburn, Martin Olliff said that President Draughon led API "through a turbulent period of growth and change." He expanded the "mission from an emphasis on the traditional land-grant role to providing undergraduate and graduate education for a complex world. He oversaw the erection of 50 buildings, the doubling of on-campus housing, the inauguration of 16 doctoral programs, as well as the accreditation of the university and of individual programs from their respective organizations by the Southern Association of Colleges and Schools, and the increase to more than 40 percent of faculty with terminal degrees."[20]

After his retirement, Dr. Draughon had an office in the Ralph Brown Draughon Library, where he had planned to write a history of Auburn. This work went unfinished, however. In 1968, at the age of sixty-eight, Ralph Draughon suffered a massive heart attack and died. President and Mrs. Draughon, who lived in Auburn until January 2005, are both buried at Pine Hill Cemetery in Auburn.

In the small den of the President's Home, the Draughon family poses for the Alabama Polytechnic Institute photographer, 1949. (Auburn University Special Collections)

First Lady Caroline Draughon in the kitchen with butler Jim Smith, 1950s. (Auburn University Special Collections)

President Ralph Draughon, First Lady Caroline, and their children, Ann and Ralph Jr., occupied the President's Home from 1948 to 1965. (Auburn University Special Collections)

Mrs. Draughon entertains in the President's Home, 1950s. (Auburn University Special Collections)

Mrs. Draughon stands in front of the Caroline Draughon Village in 1965. (Auburn University Special Collections)

President and Mrs. Draughon with the dean of home economics, Dana Gatchell, 1950s. (Auburn University Special Collections)

Caroline Draughon at the Draughon cabin on Lake Martin, early 1960s. (Courtesy of Ralph Draughon Jr.)

On the front porch of the President's Home in 1965, Dr. and Mrs. Draughon stand with their children and grandchildren. (Auburn University Special Collections)

At the President's Home where they had spent the past seventeen years, the Draughons greet the Philpotts in 1965. (Auburn University Special Collections)

On leaving the President's Home, Dr. and Mrs. Draughon spend quiet moments in the formal garden reflecting on their years of service to Auburn University. (Auburn University Special Collections)

CHAPTER FIVE

The Philpotts
1965–1980

Harry Melvin Philpott was born on May 6, 1917, in Bassett, Virginia, and was raised in Lexington, North Carolina. He graduated cum laude from Washington and Lee University in 1938. His major field of study was religion and higher education, with extensive work in philosophy and psychology. Dr. Philpott received a Ph.D. from Yale University in 1947 and his D.D. from Stetson University in 1960. He met his future wife. Polly, when both were students at Yale.

Pauline "Polly" Moran was born in Nyack, New York, on December 12, 1915. Her father was a Presbyterian minister and served as chaplain at Cornell University. Polly received a B.S. from Cornell in 1938 and a B.D. from Yale Divinity in 1941. Having lived in Switzerland for some time as a child, Polly spoke fluent French, and during the summer she spent in Canada after graduating from Cornell, she delivered sermons in French.

Harry and Polly were married in Riverside Church in New York City in 1943. Upon completion of his service as chaplain with the U.S. Navy in the Pacific during World War II, Dr. Philpott joined the faculty of the University of Florida as professor of religion, organizing there the Religion in Life Program, which received a Freedom Foundation award. After serving five years as dean of religious life in the Department of Religion and Philosophy at Stephens College,

Dr. Philpott returned to the University of Florida, where he began serving as vice-president in November 1957.

On May 13, 1966, Harry Melvin Philpott was inaugurated eleventh president of the institution and first president of Auburn University. Perhaps Providence had decreed that the first president of the new Auburn University (AU) should be a Baptist minister, just as the first president of the new land-grant college at Auburn, Alabama Agricultural and Mechanical, had been. (In 1872, Isaac Taylor Tichenor, a Baptist minister "and a staunch advocate of the scientific study of agriculture," was chosen as third president of the college at Auburn.)[1]

Dr. Philpott was selected by the trustees in May 1965 and began his tenure at Auburn that September. The announcement of his selection was made by AU trustee Frank Samford and Alabama Governor George Wallace, who said that Dr. Philpott "was well qualified to head the University because of his educational background and his experience as first vice president of the University of Florida which is a land-grant institution." Philpott's liberal-arts background worried some people in the College of Agriculture and the Extension Service, however.

On accepting the position, Dr. Philpott said he had been particularly impressed by Auburn's school spirit and that his wife and children were "looking forward to coming to Auburn."[2] When the family arrived, they brought four children, several pets, and the breeziness of Florida. An air-conditioning system was installed in the President's Home, and the screened back porch was turned into a Florida room with jalousie windows. On the eve of their father's inauguration, the children were interviewed on the "newly enclosed porch" by the *Lee County Bulletin*.

The Philpotts' oldest son, Melvin, was a sophomore at Yale, and their oldest daughter, Jeanne Todd, was a junior at Auburn High School. The younger Philpott children were son Cabell, a seventh grader, and daughter Virginia ("Gingy"), a ten-year-old fifth grader. Melvin was singing with a college group called the Spizzwinds; Jeanne, who loved sports, was planning to teach synchronized swimming at

Brevard in the summer; Cabell was playing tackle on the undefeated Auburn Junior High football team; and Gingy was taking piano and violin lessons.[3]

In the first year of the Philpott presidency, the perspective from the President's Home was extended all the way to Montgomery. Auburn University at Montgomery (AUM) was established in the middle of the cotton fields of the former McLemore Plantation east of Montgomery near Mitylene. Tensions were created both in Auburn and in the city government of Montgomery by the establishment of this branch of the Auburn University campus. Karla Davis states that this may have been "the most controversial episode in Philpott's tenure":

> In early 1967, Auburn agreed to open a branch campus in Montgomery, pending appropriation of funds from the legislature. On September 8, 1967, Governor Lurleen B. Wallace signed the Montgomery college bill. This legislation authorized $5 million worth of bonds to be applied to the establishment of Auburn University at Montgomery. . . . [The Alabama State Teachers Association (ASTA)] filed a lawsuit, expressing the belief that the construction of AUM was an attempt to further perpetuate the dual educational system in the state. Philpott insisted AUM would not be segregated and promised full cooperation with Montgomery's historically black college, Alabama State. . . . A three-judge district court ruled against the Alabama State Teachers Association's claim in 1968, . . . The case was appealed to the United States Supreme Court, which upheld the lower court's ruling. Undaunted, ASTA filed another suit claiming that legislative act 403, which approved the financing of AUM, was unconstitutional. Circuit judge Eugene Carter ruled that act 403 was constitutional, and the Alabama Supreme Court upheld his decision. AUM officially opened September 16, 1969.[4]

After the passage of the Civil Rights Act in 1964, radical changes had been mandated for all agricultural programs supported by federal funds, but the merger of the Alabama Agricultural Extension Services at the two racially segregated land-grant institutions of Alabama—

the Agricultural and Mechanical College near Huntsville in northern Alabama and Auburn University—had not gotten past the planning stage. In 1969, however, a serious legal challenge to the dual system was brought to the federal courts by Willie L. Strain of the Extension Services at Tuskegee, who had failed to be considered for an open position with Extension Services at Auburn. "President Harry Philpott was a perennial defendant in the ongoing Strain v. Harry Philpott, Auburn University lawsuits."[5] The integration of the Extension Services at Auburn did begin in 1969, and radical changes had been made over the years; but it would be 2006 before all aspects of the *Strain v. Philpott* suit, which became the class-action desegregation suit for higher education in the state of Alabama, would be settled.

Across Samford Hall from the President's Home occupied in 1973 by the Philpott family, Swingle Hall was named for Homer S. Swingle, "the father of fisheries" at Auburn University.[6]

When Polly Philpott became the First Lady of Auburn University, she assumed the duties associated with the daytime and evening events held at the President's Home that Mrs. Draughon had begun. Mrs. Philpott served as president of the Dames Club, hosting the meetings, assisting with the refreshments, planning the programs, guiding the group's projects, and presiding over the awarding of the "diplomas" these young wives received upon the graduation of their husbands.

In 2006 a former member of the Dames Club spoke to the author about the meetings hosted by Polly Philpott: "No pant suits or slacks [were allowed]. We dressed up in what would be our Sunday best. There were teas, and monthly meetings, more as a reason to support and comfort one another as most of us were working wives while Pushing Hubby Through. . . . Our diploma certificates [were] signed by Mrs. Philpott, President . . . and Mrs. Evelyn Jordan [wife of coach Ralph Jordan] Vice President. We had a service project each year [such as] raising funds to purchase little red wagons . . . to carry children to X-Ray and the operating room [at the Lee County Hospital]."[7]

In her spare time, Mrs. Philpott enjoyed reading, growing orchids, knitting, and embroidery. She had a special tablecloth on which she collected the names of the prominent guests who visited the President's Home, embroidering over these signatures in her spare time. She and her husband both loved sports and attended most of Auburn's football, basketball, and baseball games. They subscribed to several national newspapers, and Polly is remembered for simply moving stacks of newspapers aside and sharing stories of life in the President's Home with her guests.

On the fifth year of the Philpott presidency, the *Plainsman* featured the Philpott family in its May 14, 1971, edition. The photographs and commentary of this article reflect the changing times at Auburn: "Pres. Harry M. Philpott spent the afternoon of his birthday in Samford Park May 6, 'rapping' with a small and constantly shifting group of students about University policies concerning campus issues such as discipline, parking areas, outdoor loudspeakers, and dispensation of birth control pills."[8]

The Auburn University campus had also changed physically during the first five years of the Philpott administration. Memorial Coliseum, Haley Center, two veterinary medicine buildings, and two women's dormitories were constructed. Cliff Hare Stadium and the Forestry Building were also expanded. By the end of his presidency, Dr. Philpott would also see the beginning of a fine arts center and an addition to the Auburn Union.

On May 8, 1975, the *Plainsman* carried an interview with Mrs. Philpott, who had served Auburn as First Lady for ten years and was reflecting on her life at the President's Home. The war in Vietnam had ended, and the rules for coeds had changed dramatically. "Special campus housing rules for women, such as dormitory curfews, which had been in effect since Smith Hall became the first women's dorm in 1921," ended, and "the University discontinued regulations that might be in violation of federal guidelines against discrimination based on sex." The office of the Dean of Women was eliminated, and an assistant director of women's athletics was added. Sue Fincher, a businesswoman and graduate student, became the first woman and the first student to serve on the Auburn University Board of Trustees.[9]

Polly thought that the Auburn students in 1975 were more serious about their studies and more inclined to participate in blood drives and fund-raisers for humanitarian causes.[10]

For the Philpott family, the summer of 1975 was a time of celebration. Their oldest daughter, Jeanne, was married in the formal garden of the President's Home with her father officiating. On September 5, 1975, four hundred guests saluted Dr. Philpott on the tenth anniversary of his presidency at a banquet sponsored by the Auburn Chamber of Commerce. Many testimonials on behalf of Dr. and Mrs. Philpott were made at the banquet, and the *Auburn Bulletin* of August 31, 1975, quoted Mrs. Caroline Draughon, who described Dr. Philpott as "a very vigorous man, and very devoted to his family." The Philpotts had continued their friendship with the Draughons through the years, and Mrs. Draughon said that she and the late Dr. Draughon had "always been included in the university events, always assured that we were still part of the university."[11]

Over the years the Philpotts had many pets, including several Cavalier King Charles spaniels. The glassed back porch and the small den in the President's Home were favorite places for these pets as the children grew up and the grandchildren came to visit. On March 24, 1980, just before Polly left the President's Home, she was interviewed by the Auburn University News Bureau. She spoke of having "a lot of inherited Oriental pieces" and felt that the President's Home would be "somewhat barren" once her things were moved to the Philpotts' home on Cary Drive in Auburn. Polly had decorated the sunroom of the President's Home in "bamboo theme paper depicting actual Chinese folk tales [that she thought made] an attractive backdrop for the Oriental scrolls that were gifts to the Philpotts from an Auburn alumni group living in Taiwan." The scrolls depicted "a tiger and an eagle," both of which are AU mascots.[12]

The Philpotts were living in Azalea Place, an Auburn retirement home, when Mrs. Philpott died in 2005. In May 2007, Dr. Philpott celebrated his ninetieth birthday with his daughters and adult grandchildren, one of whom was a student at Auburn. Tragically, both sons of Dr. and Mrs. Philpott died as young men.

The Philpott family in the living room of the President's Home, 1966. *Standing:* Cabell, Jeanne, and Mel. *Seated:* Dr. and Mrs. Philpott, Gingy. (Auburn University Special Collections)

Football on the plains with President and Mrs. Jimmy Carter, 1970s. (Auburn University Special Collections)

The Philpott family and pets in the foyer of the President's Home, 1976. (Auburn University Special Collections)

Mrs. Philpott on the porch, 1978. (Auburn University Special Collections)

Dr. Philpott on the Auburn campus with students, 1970s. (Auburn University Special Collections)

In 1970, President Philpott receives an earlier version of Auburn's mascot, "Aubie," from Edward Kennedy. (Auburn University Special Collections)

Homecoming for the Philpott children and grandchildren, 1980. (Auburn University Special Collections)

Mrs. Philpott enjoys a quiet moment. (Auburn University Special Collections)

Dr. Philpott relaxes in the den. (Auburn University Special Collections)

CHAPTER SIX

The Funderburks

1980–1983

Hanly Funderburk and Helen Hanson were both from the rural Pickens County town of Carrollton, Alabama. After graduating from the county high school in 1949, Hanly came to Alabama Polytechnic Institute to study agriculture and graduated in 1953 with a B.S. in agricultural science. The Funderburks were married in 1953, and 2nd Lieutenant and Mrs. Funderburk spent the first two years of their marriage in the U.S. Army. After he completed his military service, the Funderburks moved back to Auburn, where Hanly completed his M.S. in botany at API. In 1961 he earned his Ph.D. in plant physiology from Louisiana State University.

The Funderburks returned to Auburn in 1962 with their young children, Debra Elaine, five, and Kenneth Cliff, one. Dr. Funderburk began his teaching and research career in the College of Agriculture at Auburn University. He was soon named assistant dean of the Graduate School, however, and he guided the planning and development of Auburn University at Montgomery during the last years of the Draughon administration.

Under President Harry Philpott in 1968, Dr. Funderburk was appointed vice-president and chief administrative officer of AUM, and in 1978 he became chancellor of the new, independent branch of Auburn University. Dr. Funderburk's leadership skills where well known by Auburn's Board of Trustees, but when Dr. Philpott retired in 1980, there were five nominations for the presidency, four of whom were Auburn graduates, including future Auburn president James Martin. The fifth was Steven Sample, executive vice-president for academic affairs at the University of Nebraska, who would become president of the University of Southern California.

Dr. Funderburk was nominated for the job by trustee Henry Steagall II of Montgomery, who believed Funderburk's "fine academic background in agriculture" and his leadership at AUM made him the perfect candidate; however, the selection process dragged on for seven months. Dr. Funderburk was finally selected on a vote of ten to one.[1]

His selection as president on April 9, 1980, ended a bitter fight over who would become Auburn's twelfth president, but it was just the beginning of a turbulent three years for Alabama's land-grant university. The political maneuvering that had accompanied the selection process served to polarize the faculty and Auburn friends across the state. Faculty distrust of the new administration quickly led to campus unrest, and this climate would force Dr. Funderburk to resign in 1983.

When he assumed the presidency of Auburn University, Dr. Funderburk made the funding problems and budget issues facing the university his first priority. State funding had been prorated, and there was a need to reduce spending and eliminate some positions, which Funderburk hoped to do through attrition.

The President's Home was in need of some renovation, and the trustees asked Mrs. Funderburk to oversee this effort, which she says she gladly did before the family moved to Auburn from Montgomery. Budget constraints kept the changes modest: some furniture was reupholstered, the kitchen and one bathroom were brought more up to date, and some wallpaper was added. All the work was done by employees of the AU Facilities Division.

Grace Jones of the *Auburn Bulletin* interviewed Mrs. Funderburk in September 1980 and reported that Helen seemed "completely at ease in the beautifully re-decorated President's home." She was faced with "a mansion of activities," however, and in her first few months as First Lady she had already hosted "two receptions for graduating seniors, their parents and friends." Helen had also completed the planning for the annual freshman picnic to be held on the lawn of the President's Home. She was expecting seventeen hundred guests on September 22 and was also working with a committee to plan the "annual fall faculty reception that would be held in the President's Home in October."[2]

When asked how she felt about her husband's being president of Auburn, Helen replied: "It is certainly a challenge and he is thrilled with it." She wondered, though, if she and her husband would have any time to play golf, a sport they both enjoyed. They had spent most of the summer visiting Auburn alumni groups in Alabama, Florida, and Georgia, and Helen expected to have lots of company during the fall football season of 1980.[3]

In 2006 Mrs. Funderburk reflected on the three years she spent in the President's Home: "I guess one of the most interesting things that happened during the first year that we were at Auburn was hiring a football coach. My husband and the trustees were interviewing during the Thanksgiving holidays, before the big Auburn-Alabama game. We had our extended family in Auburn for Thanksgiving, and were trying to have dinner. Reporters were actually climbing trees around the house, trying to see if there was a prospective football coach there. The doorbell rang multiple times during dinner. We coped as best we could, but it was an interesting time."[4]

The candidate hired was Pat Dye, whose teams would win four Southeastern Conference championship games and nine bowl games during his twelve-year career at Auburn. All-American players such as Heisman Trophy winner Bo Jackson in 1985 and Lombardi Award winner Tracy Rocker in 1988 played for Dye. To the great delight of Auburn fans, Dye's teams also defeated the Crimson Tide of the University of Alabama four consecutive years.

When he had been selected, Coach Dye and his wife joined the Funderburks and AU trustees for a dinner at the President's Home that included former president Gerald Ford, who had come to Auburn to speak at a conference held by Auburn University students. For Mrs. Funderburk, "the real experience was having the Secret Service in the kitchen checking out the food. President Ford was most gracious and the people traveling with him were very polite and respectful of the private dinner."[5]

Another U.S. president, George H. W. Bush, also spent time on the Auburn campus during the Funderburk administration. According to Mrs. Funderburk, Bush came "for a football game while he was running for office. Unfortunately, he was stung by a bee while watching the game, was allergic to bee stings, and had to be rushed to the doctor." (Bush was not elected president of the U.S. until November 1988, but he had campaigned for the Republican nomination received by Ronald Reagan in 1980.)

By October 1980 Mrs. Funderburk was well seasoned to the entertaining required of her at Auburn; she was very proud of having had "the biggest crowd ever at the freshman picnic" held on the lawn of the President's Home in September. She gave credit for its success to the university's Facilities Department and expressed a desire to continue with all the traditional events of Auburn University and to add more small-group faculty dinners to her responsibilities. Auburn had a much larger faculty than AUM, but Mrs. Funderburk wanted to become as personally acquainted with the AU faculty as she had been with those at AUM, where she had been able to have the entire faculty to her home for dinner.[6]

In spite of her preference for entertaining small groups, Mrs. Funderburk was most often called upon to entertain large groups at Auburn University. At times she had to suspend her private life for duties as Auburn's official hostess, such as when the birth of her first grandchild was pending. In the spring of 1981, Mrs. Funderburk was giving a large party on the lawn of the President's Home "to introduce Mrs. Pat Dye, the new football coach's wife, to the community" when she got the call that her daughter had gone into labor.

Christmas 1981 at the President's Home was especially nice for the Funderburks with a visit from their new granddaughter, Ashley Lynn Dahl. Mrs. Funderburk remembered that the ornaments for the tree at the President's Home that year had been designed and made by Gary Trentham, a professor in textile designs, and that *Southern Living* magazine, published in Birmingham by Auburn graduates, featured the tree in its Christmas issue the next year.

In 1982, Auburn graduates Ken Mattingly and Hank Hartsfield took AU into space aboard the shuttle *Columbia*. The Funderburks felt fortunate to be invited to watch the launch from Cape Kennedy, and Mrs. Funderburk recalled that later "the two astronauts visited us in Auburn, attended a football game, and presented Hanly a beautiful picture with a small American flag" that had been taken with the astronauts into space.[7]

President Funderburk remained upbeat in his message to the faculty at the end of 1982 despite a deteriorating situation partially caused by the protest resignations of members of the faculty, including two vice-presidents, and a no-confidence vote by the Faculty Senate. "We are making every effort to involve people throughout the region in the years ahead," he said. "Our own outlook is optimistic, but there remain many challenges before us. The desired excellence we hope to achieve will require the fullest support of all our leaders and we will work tirelessly toward that goal."[8]

When the Funderburks left Auburn in February 1983, "the university was financially sound, and the capital campaign, begun fiscal year 1979–80, had grown to nearly $42 million of its $62 million goal."

As president of Auburn University, Dr. Funderburk enjoyed walking almost every day on the Auburn campus. He continued this habit as president of Eastern Kentucky University, where he served until his retirement. He also enjoyed working outside in the yard of his personal home.[9]

Although the campus scene from the porch of the President's Home did not change physically during the Funderburk administration, Dr. Funderburk "left an active construction program primed for better economic times in Alabama higher education."[10]

Dr. and Mrs. Funderburk with children Kenneth and Debra and son-in-law, Jim Dahl, 1980. (Auburn University Special Collections)

Helen Funderburk, First Lady of Auburn University, September 1980. (Auburn University Special Collections)

At a board dinner, Dr. and Mrs. Funderburk also host a new coach. (Courtesy of Helen Funderburk)

The Funderburks with Gerald Ford in the foyer of the President's Home, 1980. (Auburn University Special Collections)

In the president's open "sky box" for Auburn football, 1980s. (Auburn University Special Collections)

Christmas in the President's Home with the Funderburks' first grandchild, 1981. (Courtesy of Helen Funderburk)

The Funderburks receive astronauts Ken Mattingly and Hank Hartsfield, 1982. (Auburn University Special Collections)

CHAPTER SEVEN

The Baileys
1983–1984

On March 1, 1983, Dr. Wilford Bailey, former vice-president for academic affairs during the Philpott administration, assumed the responsibilities of the president of Auburn University. He had been recruited from retirement and had agreed to serve until a new president for Auburn University could be found.

In 1938 Wil Bailey came to Auburn with his mother and brothers from Hartselle, Alabama. His father, a northern Alabama farmer, had died during the hard times of the Great Depression, and his mother had sold the family farm and moved to Auburn, where she ran a boardinghouse in order to send her sons to the renowned School of Veterinary Medicine at Alabama Polytechnic Institute. According to Yeager and Stevenson “The list of faculty who came to Auburn during the years when William LeRoy Broun was president includes some truly outstanding scientists. . . . Charles A. Cary (D.V.M., B.S.), who brought physiology and veterinary medicine to the agricultural curriculum in 1893 and who headed Auburn’s first organized outreach efforts (Farmers’ Institutes), later became the first Dean of Veterinary Medicine at Auburn.”[1]

Cratus “Kate” Hester was born in 1916 in a Franklin County log cabin at Dodd Hollow and grew up wanting to be a home demonstration agent with the Extension Service in Cullman County. She had wanted to come to Auburn as a teen, but her father insisted that she go first to David Lipscomb College and then to Peabody College, from which she graduated in 1940.

Kate met her future husband in the summer of 1940 in Auburn at the Church of Christ on Glenn Avenue. Wil was a veterinary student at API, and Kate had come to the college that summer to take the extra courses required for a job with the Extension Service.

According to Joe Yeager and Gene Stevenson in *Inside Ag Hill,* "Assisting Alabama farm families in areas of family living was an immediate priority when the Extension Service was organized. In fact, the agency was listed as Junior and Home Economics Extension Department until the College's 1920–21 Bulletin changed it to Agricultural Extension Service. That listing of State staff included five involved in Women's Work: Mary Feminear, State Home Demonstration Agent, and Helen Johnston, Mina Willis, May Cureton, and Elizabeth Mauldin, Assistant State Home Demonstration Agents."[2]

In the summer of 1940, Kate Hester waited tables at Auburn Grill to pay for her courses and expenses at Auburn. Every morning she served her future boss unaware; and as a tip to the waitress, the director of the Farm Security Administration in Cullman County left Kate a quarter. In the fall, Kate was hired and "loved every minute" of her job working with the low-income farm families of northern Alabama. "It was my joy," Mrs. Bailey said in 2006, "to help these people fill out forms for government-subsidized farm loans." She also taught the women on these farms how to use a pressure cooker, how to preserve food from their gardens, how to make clothes from feed sacks, how to cull out chickens not laying, and how to rid their homes of fleas. Kate's compassion for the struggling farmers of northern Alabama and her hard work earned her the respect and admiration of those she served. Her memories of these people are among those she treasures most; but Kate's career days were also filled with letters from Wil Bailey, who begged her to return to Auburn and marry him. This she did in the spring of 1942.

After graduating from the School of Veterinary Medicine in 1942, Wilford Bailey began his career teaching at API. In 1948 the Baileys and their two young sons, Joe and Edward, moved to Maryland, where Wil earned a Doctorate of Science from Johns Hopkins University. Their daughters, Margaret and Sarah, soon completed the large family Mrs. Bailey had always wanted. The family returned to Auburn, where they lived throughout Dr. Bailey's long career with Auburn University.

When Dr. Bailey accepted the job of interim president of Auburn University in 1983, Kate felt that moving into the President's Home was unnecessary given the brevity of their intended stay. Her acceptance of the social responsibilities of the First Lady, however, compelled her to spend some time in the "mansion" she had known as the home of the Draughons and the Philpotts. "There was nothing at the President's Home that belonged to me except my toothbrush and pajamas," she said in 2006, "but our special treat was to spend the Christmas week of '83 there with our whole family."[3]

For a Christmas 1983 snapshot (see gallery) the Bailey family gathered in the sunroom and sat on the rattan furniture purchased by Caroline Draughon in 1949. Although Dr. Bailey did not take this picture of himself and his family, "photography became his hobby" when he used cameras "for about fifty-five years in his career in pathology and parasitology." Dr. Bailey had made "thousands of slides on research-related trips to about forty countries, including China, Poland, Egypt, Greece, and Australia."[4]

Mrs. Bailey remembered that the Christmas of 1983 was extremely cold in Auburn, and that the Baileys' holiday spirit was slightly chilled that night at the President's Home: "During this time . . . the temperature was 7 degrees and the fountains on campus froze in mid air!! Also we were unaware that a basement window was broken and almost gone, leaving [freezing] weather coming [into the President's home]. . . . With all 16 of us in the house our water pipes froze. We had no water anywhere in the house, but with B&G [Buildings and Grounds, now the Facilities Department] things returned to normal."

In spite of the cold and lack of water, Mrs. Bailey thought the President's Home looked beautiful that Christmas. "Our Christmas tree was decorated by Emily Leischuck & Stanley Sistrunk. It was most beautiful [and] all I had to do was sit and enjoy it. . . . It was wonderful to have enough beds, bathrooms, dining space and kitchen help to take care of meals, supervise grandchildren and cut their food for them."[5]

In the year they served Auburn University as president and First Lady, Dr. and Mrs. Bailey carried out the responsibilities of their positions with dignity and grace. Their year of service to Auburn has been lovingly preserved in a scrapbook made by their daughter-in-law Marsha.

On March 16, 1984, Dr. Wilford Bailey was awarded a doctorate and the title of thirteenth president of Auburn University. Auburn's newly appointed fourteenth president, James Martin, conveyed the gratitude of the greater "Auburn family" in Memorial Coliseum, saying that Dr. Bailey had performed "with exceptional merit in a variety of positions both within the University's program of teaching and research and within the institution's administrative structure."[6]

Dr. Bailey's service to Auburn University included his duties as vice-chairman of the Office of Research and Graduate Studies and associate dean for Research and Graduate Studies in the School (now College) of Veterinary Medicine. During his tenure as president he worked to raise money for scholarships at Auburn and for teaching and research equipment. He assisted Dr. Martin in the transition of his administration to Martin's, and he served a four-year term as a member of the National Collegiate Athletic Association Council.[7]

A young Wilford Bailey in his lab at Alabama Polytechnic Institute. (Auburn University Special Collections)

Dr. and Mrs. Bailey and their children: Joe and Edward, Sarah and Margaret, 1983. (Courtesy of Cratus Bailey)

The freshman picnic at the President's Home, fall 1983. (Auburn University Special Collections)

The Baileys spend Christmas in the President's Home, 1983. (Courtesy of Cratus Bailey)

CHAPTER EIGHT

The Martins
1984–1992

Jim and Ann Martin met in Auburn in 1953 when they were students at API. James E. Martin was born in Cullman County in 1932 and grew up in Greensboro, Alabama. He came to Auburn on a four-year athletic scholarship and earned a B.S. in agricultural management. Ann Freeman was born in Birmingham in 1935 and came to Auburn to study home economics and (by her own admission) to find a husband. She found Jim playing center on the API basketball team when she joined the cheerleading squad.

When Jim graduated in 1954, he left Ann to finish her education while he completed his military service with the U.S. Army. In 1958 he earned an M.S. in agricultural economics from North Carolina State University and married Ann. They went to Iowa State University, where Jim had an assistantship to work on his doctorate in agricultural economics.

In 1962 the Martins moved to the University of Maryland with Mike, the first of their three children. Dr. Martin began his career as an agribusiness teacher at Oklahoma State University, where Ann says he loved teaching. In 1968, however, Jim gave up teaching and became dean of the College of Agriculture and Life Sciences at Virginia Polytechnic Institute. In 1975 the Martins moved with their three children—Mike, Jill, and Bill—to Arkansas, where Dr. Martin's administrative career accelerated, taking him from vice-president of agriculture to chancellor of the University of Arkansas system by 1980.

He had been a candidate for the president's job at AU when Hanly Funderburk was selected, and in 1984 Jim Martin accepted the presidency of Auburn University.

When the Martins moved to Auburn in April 1984, all the news articles reported that they were a team who had returned to their alma mater. Comparisons were made between the two, who were said to be "distinctly individual, even though each exhibits the same spontaneity and affableness around new acquaintances." The big difference between Jim (six foot six) and Ann (five foot three) was their height. They both enjoyed going to plays and symphonies and taking long walks together around the campus "four nights a week."[1]

A week before his inauguration in May 1984, Dr. Martin was interviewed by Kaye Lovvorn, editor of the *Auburn Alumnews,* who reported that he was impressed with the campus and with the student enrollment, both of which had tripled since he was a student at API. Dr. Martin praised the breadth of the programs offered, the dedication of the faculty, and the high ACT scores of the students. He believed there was "untapped potential" at Auburn and that people were interested in "Auburn's academic programs—the teaching, research, and public service programs." He hoped to increase faculty salaries and to provide additional funding for the College of Arts and Sciences and the Ralph Brown Draughon Library. He also wanted "to improve the number of minorities and women on both our faculty and in our student body." (The new president of Auburn was addressing many of the complaints that had been brought against Auburn by the faculty and others.) For his personal enrichment, Dr. Martin hoped to have a home computer in the President's Home and to master this new technology.[2]

In the next eight years, President Martin accomplished many of the goals he set for Auburn University; he was also involved in several controversies. The one that the faculty felt was most contradictory to his expressed desire to make Auburn University the kind of place eminent scholars would be drawn to was the Curran affair. This resulted in the denial of an eminent scholar's chair to a controversial Catholic priest and may have influenced Martin's decision to retire.[3] This came at the end of the Martin administration, however. At the beginning of his presidency, according to Yeager and Stevenson, Jim Martin started a storm of controversy on Ag Hill:

> Politics of the Martin years centered around a controversial administrative reorganization that most Ag Hill faculty and Alabama agricultural leaders saw as not only reducing emphasis on agriculture but which would violate the historical organization and operation of agricultural teaching, research, and extension programs under provisions of the Morrill, Hatch, and Smith-Lever Acts. The new organization, proposed by a campus committee that was chaired by Executive Vice-President George Emert, was accepted by Martin as a way to increase efficiency and allow Auburn to better serve its mission.[4]

Dr. Martin seems to have been able to leave the business of running the university at Samford Hall and to enjoy his hobbies. He kept up his health and energy by shooting baskets on the basketball goal he had installed at the President's Home and by tinkering with the three Ford Thunderbirds he owned during his presidency.

The repercussions of Dr. Martin's changes in the College of Agriculture and the Extension Service did cause major headaches and hostility toward Auburn's fourteenth president, but in 1994 President Martin was honored to be a part of the College of Agriculture's "milestone in fisheries." In New York City, the United Nations "announced the establishment of an international network headquartered at Auburn for communicating fisheries information around the world." Dr. Martin and Wayne Shell "led an Auburn delegation that appeared at the press conference and interacted with foreign journalists who covered the world. This event was held the same week that Auburn's football team played in the 'Kickoff Classic' at the Meadowlands, thereby reminding the world that Auburn was much more than just a football factory."[5]

Among the many accomplishments of his administration, Dr. Martin initiated the program of issuing special Auburn University car tags to raise revenue. In 2006 revenue from the Auburn tag sales approached $20 million.

Dr. Martin was also proud of having taught himself to play the piano. In an interview with the *Auburn Bulletin,* he said: "It's all mathematic. You pick out a note and maintain three keys, two black and one white. You change keys by shifting everything up or down."[6] According to those who visited the President's Home when the Martins were meeting the social requirements of the presidency, Dr. Martin sometimes used his skill at the piano to send a gentle message. He would begin playing the piano when the events of the evening began to drag on, and everyone came to realize that this was the signal to leave.

It is doubtful however that Dr. Martin played the piano during the wedding reception held in the President's Home for his only daughter Jill, who married in 1986. Family affairs continued to be part of life in the President's Home, and the Martins became grandparents in 1988 when their granddaughter, Taylor RayAnn Richmond, was born on the Fourth of July. Mrs. Martin joked that the family had planned to call the baby "firecracker."

During the eight years of the Martins' residence in the President's Home, Mrs. Martin hosted many events for the trustees and other members of the faculty and administration as well as the larger Auburn community. Her charm and hospitality are well remembered. She also enjoyed handicrafts and kept the butler's pantry in the President's Home filled with ribbons, wrappings, and colorful things used to make special gifts for social events and favorite friends.

Before the Martins left the President's Home in March 1992, a farewell party was held for them. The *Auburn Alumnews* reported the event in an article titled "Martins Bid Fond Farewell." They had come on Valentine's Day in 1984, and on February 29, 1992, "more than 500 alumni, faculty, staff, and students crowded the Auburn University Hotel and Conference Center" to pay tribute to President and Mrs. Martin.

When the Martins came to live in the President's Home in 1984, the campus seemed completely different than it had been in their student days at Auburn. On their retirement from Auburn University in

1992, the campus was again changed dramatically. In addition to the $20.5 million expansion of the Ralph Brown Draughon Library, they had witnessed the construction of a new alumni center, the new John M. Harbert Engineering Center, the Auburn Hotel and Conference Center, an aerospace engineering center, an athletic center, and the east upper deck of Jordan-Hare Stadium.[7]

Dr. and Mrs. Martin in the President's Home with their children, Jill, Bill, and Mike, 1984. (Auburn University Special Collections)

Dr. Martin greets students at Auburn, 1984. (Auburn University Special Collections)

President Jim Martin gets his Auburn tag, 1989. (Auburn University Special Collections)

The Martins in the sunroom of the President's Home, 1984. (Auburn University Special Collections)

Wedding day for President and Mrs. Martin's daughter, Jill, 1986. (Auburn University Special Collections)

Photograph of the Better Relations Day event held at the President's Home when the Auburn v. Alabama football classic was played in Jordan-Hare Stadium for the first time, November 1989. (Auburn University Special Collections)

CHAPTER NINE

The Muses

1992–2001

On March 1, 1992, Dr. William Van Muse was inaugurated fifteenth president of Auburn University. He was born in Marks, Mississippi, in 1939 and grew up on a Mississippi Delta farm, one of seven sons of a Church of God minister. Bill Muse had played baseball "from Little League through high school and college and into the semipro ranks."[1] He went to college on a baseball scholarship and earned his B.S. in accounting from Northwestern Louisiana State University in 1960. From there he went to the University of Arkansas, earning an M.B.A. in 1961 and a Ph.D. in business administration in 1966.

Marlene Munden was born in Scottsburg, Indiana, in 1945. She met Bill when both were working at the national headquarters of his fraternity, Tau Kappa Epsilon. They were married in 1965. Dr. and Mrs. William Van Muse came to Auburn from Akron, Ohio, where Bill had served as president of Akron University for almost eight years. The Muses had been married for twenty-seven years when they came to Auburn, and Mrs. Muse had raised her three children and completed her college education. She had also been active in humanitarian organizations such as Habitat for Humanity.

When the Muses moved into the President's Home, their children were gainfully employed college graduates. Amy, twenty-six, had graduated from the University of Akron and was working for the St. Paul Chamber Orchestra; Ellen, twenty-four, a graduate of Worcester

State College, was a counselor in Worchester, Massachusetts; William Van Jr. held a degree from Ohio University and worked in Cleveland. The Muses moved into the "mansion" with only their little "Scottie" and two cats. The first three months at Auburn were "a hectic sprint" for Bill and Marlene Muse.

In his inaugural address, Dr. Muse spoke of his goals for the university. He wanted to make Auburn more "responsible to the needs of the constituency that it served." He believed that Auburn "should remain true to its mission as a land-grant university."[2]

Three years after assuming the presidency at Auburn, Dr. Muse found himself facing the university's worst financial crisis since that faced by Dr. Funderburk in the early 1980s. Being perhaps aware of the criticisms others before him had taken on the lack of faculty involvement "in matters affecting them," Muse said he wanted to "carefully, methodically, and collegially . . . determine how best to use what is available, in order to protect the instructional quality that has become characteristic of Auburn University." In deciding how to spend money, Muse asked that the faculty rank academic and administrative programs on "undergraduate instruction and other key elements of the University's mission."[3] He had found that many of the degree programs at Auburn did not have the graduates necessary to meet the viability standards, and he recommended their elimination.

In order to study the problem further, however, Dr. Muse created a commission of faculty and administrators to study the problem and make recommendations. This 21st Century Review Commission recommended that a provost position be established to oversee the research mission of Auburn's Extension Services and other outreach programs. In 1993, Dr. Paul Parks became the first to fill this position. Dr. Parks had come to Auburn in 1965 as a faculty member in the Department of Animal and Dairy Sciences, and in 1972 he was appointed dean of the Graduate School by President Philpott. In restructuring the Extension Service, Dr. Martin had selected Dr. Parks as the full-time vice-president of research. When Dr. Muse moved Dr. Parks into Samford Hall as provost and vice-president of research, however, many in the agriculture and engineering departments were unhappy over the loss of the "authority of the [Agricultural Experiment] Station Director in funds allocation, faculty hiring, and planning and carrying out of research."[4]

Before Dr. and Mrs. Muse moved into the President's Home, Marlene was welcomed to Auburn with a luncheon given by Mrs. Emily Leischuck, who had served as coordinator of events in the president's office since the Bailey administration. The luncheon for Mrs. Muse at the home of Mrs. Leischuck included Mrs. Caroline Draughon, Mrs. Polly Philpott, Mrs. Kate Bailey, and Mrs. Ann Martin. This event was a first, with four of the previous six First Ladies welcoming Mrs. Muse, wife of Auburn's fifteenth president.

Marlene Muse was featured in the "Life/Style" section of the *Birmingham News* on Sunday, April 12, 1992. She spoke about her husband's philosophy of being happy with "who you are, and where you are." She talked about her children and said that daughter Amy had suggested that her parents offer a football weekend in Auburn as a prize for one of the benefits she was working on for the St. Paul Orchestra. Amy had been contacted by the Auburn alumni chapter of Minneapolis, who called themselves the "Frozen Eagles" (a pun on the Auburn chant "War Eagle"), about staging such an event.

In the interview, Mrs. Muse addressed the campus issue of the day, sexual discrimination and gay rights, and said she believed that if those who were pushing to be acknowledged as a legitimate campus organization agreed to follow the rules set for other groups, they should be considered as just another organization. She said that we "are all God's people, and we understand very little about homosexuality."[5]

Politics of all sorts caused continual stress at Auburn during the Muse administration. When he arrived in 1992, Dr. Muse faced the on-campus politics caused by the "Old South" parade held annually by Kappa Alpha fraternity. Many students felt the parade was a racist reminder of slavery, and when violence nearly erupted during a protest against the event, Dr. Muse and members of the Student Government Association persuaded the fraternity to discontinue it.[6]

Fortunately, Auburn campus politics did not prompt this shocking headline: "Ablaze: 55-Year-Old President's Mansion Ignited by

Maintenance Accident." But for Dr. and Mrs. Muse, the headaches caused by the fire of May 1994 lasted nearly a year. Mrs. Muse and her "Scottie" were alone in the house on the afternoon when she was notified by the painters that the attic was on fire. An AU employee passing the house at the time called 911 on her car phone, and within minutes of receiving the 3:15 p.m. call the Auburn firefighters arrived. The damage was estimated at $150,000, and the repairs were supposed to take between 90 and 120 days. The attic was charred, and the fire and water caused damage on the second floor; but the collection of children's books Mrs. Muse had saved from her children's childhood days survived. The Muses, however, were forced to stay at the Heart of Auburn Motel for nearly nine months.[7]

During the ordeal of living away from the President's Home in 1994, Dr. and Mrs. Muse had the pleasure of learning that the art museum project, initiated in 1992 by Dr. Muse and others and approved by the trustees, had received a significant contribution to the building fund by the Phillips family. In 1998 this gift was tripled by Albert Smith, who contributed the $3 million that made possible the Jule Collins Smith Museum of Art, named for his wife.

In 1948 the U.S. State Department had held an auction of 117 paintings as war surplus. The head of Auburn's art department at the time, Frank Applebee, heard about the auction and started collecting money from his colleagues and others to make a bid on the paintings. "Taking advantage of a 95 percent discount offered by the government to qualified purchasers, Applebee was able to purchase 36 paintings for $1,072. Described as the art bargain of the century, many of these paintings represent the finest works ever executed by such luminaries of the American art scene as Ralston Crawford, Ben Shahn, Georgia O'Keefe, John Marin, Jacob Lawrence, Arthur Dove and Romare Bearden."[8] At Alabama's land-grant college, however, there was no proper housing for the paintings, and they were hung in the offices of various administrators and professors. Some funds for a building to house this collection were provided by the Hargis Foundation during the Philpott administration, but it would be twenty years before an amount large enough to consider building a museum was made available. Dr. Muse and others worked to persuade Susan Phillips of Brewton to contribute the initial $1 million needed for the museum as well as her grandfather's collection of John James Audubon prints.

In the fall of 1995 when Dr. Ed Richardson, state superintendent of education, became an ex officio member of the AU Board of Trustees, Dr. Muse had been serving as president of Auburn University for three and a half difficult years. There had been major scandals over National Collegiate Athletics Association (NCAA) violations in men's athletics: "Pat Dye held his final news conference as Auburn's football coach on November 26, 1992, at Legion Field after Alabama beat the Tigers 17-0. Flanked by his players, he called his wife . . . and his children . . . to his side. [He] had maintained for more than a year that he had no knowledge of NCAA rules violations committed by members of his staff or boosters."[9]

Yet the violations in the football program as well as those in the men's basketball program may have seemed minor compared to the fight that was going on among the Auburn trustees and Alabama Governor Fob James. In 1995, Dr. Muse was coping with major decisions regarding the probations and sanctions placed on Auburn athletics, and he had not been given a contract by the AU Board of Trustees. Governor James was continuing his battle with the legislature over the trustees he had selected to replace longtime members whose terms had expired. During this time the AU trustees not involved in the tug-of-war assured Dr. Muse the "first written contract ever awarded an Auburn president," extending his tenure until March 1, 2002.

By 1998 when Governor Siegelman had succeeded Fob James the AU Board of Trustees had regrouped around the former trustees, and Dr. William Walker had replaced Dr. Paul Parks as provost at Auburn. On January 30, 2001, the trustees announced the removal of Dr. Muse from his position as president, saying that he would be allowed to complete his contract as an adviser to the board while a national search for a new president was being conducted. In February 2001, Bill Walker became interim president of Auburn, and Dr. Muse was moved into a small office where he finished his service to Auburn and waited to begin his new job as chancellor of East Carolina University in August 2001.

During the last months of his tenure at Auburn, Dr. Muse was interviewed by the East Carolina University newspaper, *Pieces of Eight,* and he spoke of his grandchildren whose photos stood on his desk along with a picture of himself with Hank Aaron. The Muses had been happy to have their first granddaughter, one-year-old Madelyn, living in Auburn during the past year while her parents were there pursuing graduate degrees and they were also looking forward to a visit with two-year-old grandson Henry, who lived in Cincinnati, Ohio.[10]

During the nine years that Marlene Muse served as First Lady of Auburn University, entertaining alumni, trustees, and guests, she also worked for other causes dear to her, such as Habitat for Humanity, the Lee County Boys and Girls Clubs, and Youth Development Services. Mrs. Muse was unable to accompany her husband on his introductory visit to East Carolina University because she was in charge of the silent auction to raise funds for Habitat for Humanity, and the "president's home was full of donated items that needed sorting and labeling."[11]

The Muses receive a visit from their children in the President's Home, 1992. *Left to right:* President Muse, Amy, Van, Ellen, and First Lady Marlene. (Auburn University Special Collections)

The former First Ladies of the President's Home (with the exception of Mrs. Duncan and Mrs. Funderburk) greet Mrs. Muse in the home of Emily Leischuck, 1992. (Auburn University Special Collections)

First Lady Marlene Muse, happy to be in the President's Home, 1992. (*Birmingham News*)

Working for humanitarian causes. Dr. and Mrs. Muse with Mayor Jan Dempsey and members of the Auburn Chamber of Commerce in the boardroom of Samford Hall. (Auburn University Special Collections)

CHAPTER TEN

The Walkers

2001–2003

The Walkers moved to Auburn from Houston, Texas, in 1988, when Dr. William F. Walker was selected as dean of the College of Engineering at Auburn University. They had both been born in Texas: Bill in Sherman in 1937, Myrna in Bryan in 1940. When they came to Auburn, Myrna Walker said she was "the tag-along wife" who left her adult children (daughter Audrey and son Forrest) in college and followed her husband to Auburn.

The distance between Auburn and Houston must have been too great for easy visits, however, because Audrey and Forrest soon transferred to Auburn University, from which they both graduated. In 1999, Audrey and her husband, Tom Rummele, added triplets to the family of Dr. and Mrs. Bill Walker. The Walkers remained in their Auburn home for a time after Bill was named president of Auburn University, and they were in the process of building a lovely home for their retirement years during Bill's interim presidency. In the fall of 2003, however, the Walkers were occupying the President's Home and enjoying visits from their almost four-year-old grandchildren, Matthew, Megan, and Trey. The triplets posed in play with the Auburn mascot Aubie on the lawn of the President's Home, and President and Mrs. Walker proudly presented the scene on the president's official Christmas cards of 2003.

Bill and Myrna Walker had met when they were both students at the University of Texas at Austin and were married on June 5, 1960.

Bill earned both a bachelor's degree and a master's degree in aerospace engineering at the University of Texas at Austin, and Myrna earned a B.S. in business education at the University of Texas in 1961. After Myrna's graduation, the Walkers moved to Arlington, Texas, where Bill worked in aircraft manufacturing. The Walkers soon relocated to Stillwater, Oklahoma, where Bill earned his Ph.D. in mechanical engineering at Oklahoma State University in 1965. He began his teaching career at Rice University in Houston in the fall of 1965, and remained there until he accepted the position of dean of the College of Engineering at Auburn University in 1988.

At Oklahoma State, Myrna Walker began her administrative career as secretary to the director of the Agricultural Experiment Station. After her children were born, she became a full-time mother. She returned to her career in 1974 as secretary to the vice-president of the Health Science Center in Houston's Medical Center.

When Bill Walker was chosen by the trustees to fill the brief tenure of Paul Parks as provost, he was also appointed chairman of a trustee committee that included Ed Richardson as vice-chair. This ten-member commission was set up to review the work of the faculty committee that Dr. Muse had appointed to review the structure and programs of the university. The recommendations of the trustee committee differed in several ways from the recommendations of Dr. Muse's committee. Some of those differences sparked concern in some members of the faculty, and animosity began to build among alumni as well as among those who felt they were adversely affected by the restructuring actions taken on the recommendations of the trustee committee.

In an *Auburn University News* bulletin on July 14, 1998, Roy Summerford quoted President Muse as acknowledging Dr. Walker's competence as provost in providing "continuity to our academic programs." His accomplishments as dean of the College of Engineering were also cited: Walker had "overseen successful efforts to modernize engineering facilities and programs, involve faculty in strategic planning for the college, increase the minority and female student populations to more than the national average, institute awards for quality teaching and expand the engineering curriculum to include broader exposure to the liberal arts."[1]

When Dr. Walker was tapped by the Board of Trustees to succeed Dr. Muse as interim president, the news was again reported by Roy Summerford. He quoted the board's president, Jimmy Samford: "The next few months are critical to Auburn from a budget and academic standpoint, and we need to manage the shortfall we have this year while planning for next year's budget." Thus Dr. Walker was a natural choice as interim president because of his "role as AU's chief academic officer, his experience as a faculty member and administrator and strengths he brings to the position." Samford characterized Dr. Walker as a straight shooter who "feels very strongly about Auburn University."[2]

On April 28, 2003, Dr. William F. Walker, Auburn's sixteenth president, sought to reunite the university at a formal convocation of students, faculty, staff, alumni, and board members, commenting that "History teaches us that change will take place, and I have attempted to embrace it in formulating a vision for a great university in the 21st century." He reviewed the history of disagreements among members of the "Auburn family" and said that he was thankful for the support he had received during his two years of service as interim president. He cited seven areas of progress that had been made in the short time he had been in the presidency, including the raising of faculty salaries and adhering to "the objective of keeping all members of the Auburn Family fully and accurately informed."[3]

"The hours have gone out the window," First Lady Myrna Walker said at the gala she gave for Auburn students on the lawn and in the President's Home in August 2003, but "so as long as there is food and everyone is having a good time, we will be here." Orange and blue balloons were everywhere, the food was still set out, the greeting committee was still welcoming guests at the front door, and the *Plainsman* reporter was interviewing Mrs. Walker. Amanda Holmes noted the students' appreciation for the Walkers' welcoming event. Will

Gaither, vice-president of the Student Government Association, said he thought there were perhaps a thousand participants and that "it was really generous of the President to open his house to us." But the weather became inclement, and the outdoor movie scheduled for 8:00 had to be canceled.[4]

Ginger, the Walkers' golden retriever, might not have been invited to the student open house, but for the next *Plainsman* interview Myrna and Ginger were relaxing in the sunroom in one of a pair of beautiful wingback chairs purchased perhaps by Mrs. Walker herself. First Lady Myrna's "get-the-job-done" attitude was just what it took to finally replace the worn-out and water-damaged furniture in the President's Home. She delighted the wives of the Board of Trustees one evening after dinner with a tour of the upstairs bedrooms which she had beautifully furnished.

She had worked hard, Myrna reported to the *Plainsman* in October 2003, because the President's Home and its contents were the property of the state of Alabama, and she wanted people who came to Auburn to feel welcome and proud of the President's Home. Myrna had also added wrought-iron fencing to a section of the backyard for the safety of Ginger and the triplets. To the English garden look of the yard established by Mrs. Muse, Myrna added flowering shrubs that were known for attracting butterflies. Mrs. Walker's contributions to the Auburn community were noted: "When she isn't busy with home or garden, Mrs. Walker divides her time between church, the Lee County Youth Development Board of Directors and several other community organizations," and she "likes to sew, knit and decorate when she has the time." Myrna said that she and President Walker also shared a love of jazz and the country music of George Strait.[5]

In December 2003, news of a trip involving President Walker and several trustees concerning a possible change of football coaches spread through the state media and made the national news. Under duress, Bill Walker resigned as president of Auburn University in January 2004. He returned to the classroom until his retirement the following year.

While they were living in the President's Home at Auburn University, the Walkers received many important guests. Among these were Senator and Mrs. Richard Shelby, retired representative Howell Heflin, NAACP Chairman Julian Bond, and former president of the Soviet Union Mikhail Gorbachev.

The triplet grandchildren of Bill and Myrna Walker on the lawn of the President's Home with Aubie, 2003. (Auburn University Photographic Services)

Walker granddaughter Megan guards the door, Thanksgiving 2003. (Courtesy of Myrna Walker)

Mrs. Walker shows off the hydrangeas in the garden of the President's Home. (*Auburn Plainsman*)

Dr. and Mrs. Walker with NAACP chairman Julian Bond, January 14, 2003. (Auburn University Photographic Services)

Dr. and Mrs. Walker with former Soviet Union president Mikhail Gorbachev, October 13, 2003. (Auburn University Photographic Services)

President and Mrs. Walker host a new version of the freshman picnic, August 2003. (Auburn University Photographic Services)

CHAPTER ELEVEN

The Richardsons

2004–2007

Dr. Edward R. Richardson accepted the challenges of administering Auburn University as interim president on January 16, 2004. Following the sudden resignation of AU President William Walker, the Auburn Board of Trustees appointed Dr. Richardson, then superintendent of the state's public schools, to the presidency at Auburn until the probationary status under which Auburn University had been placed could be removed.

Ed Richardson was born in Pensacola, Florida, on January 24, 1939, and moved as a young teen to the farm of his father and grandfather near Banks, Alabama. He was not happy about leaving his childhood friends in Pensacola, especially those who shared his love of tennis, but he credits the formation of his character with his years of hard work on the family farm.

Ed began his higher education near his home at the college now named Troy University, but he soon transferred to Auburn. During the time Ed was a student the name of the university changed from API to Auburn University.

Intending to earn a degree in forestry at API, Ed changed his major to science education in his senior year, though he has retained a lifelong interest in forests. Just before his graduation in 1962, Ed Richardson met and married his wife, Nell, and they became one of thousands of couples who could say of their relationship, "It began at Auburn."

Nell Campbell was born in Selma, Alabama, in March 1943 and moved to Montgomery in 1959, graduating from Sidney Lanier High School in 1961. It was 1983 before Mrs. Richardson would complete a B.S. degree in Liberal Arts, English, at Auburn University. In 1988 she earned an M.S. in English education, also at Auburn, and began a career teaching secondary English and French. In 1990 Mrs. Richardson earned a certificate for additional work in French from the University of Alabama.

In the fall of 1962, Ed Richardson began his career as a science teacher at Cloverdale Junior High School in Montgomery, where he soon became assistant principal and principal. In 1968 and in 1972, Ed earned the master's and doctorate degrees in Educational Administration from Auburn University. In 1972 Ed began an eight-year career as principal of the high school in Andalusia, Alabama, during which time he also served as adjunct instructor of graduate classes in educational leadership through the newly created branch of Auburn, AUM.

In 1980 the Richardson family returned to Montgomery, where Dr. Richardson was employed in the Department of Educational Leadership at AUM. In 1982 he accepted the position of superintendent of Auburn City Schools, and the family returned to the city of Auburn, where daughter Merit was an Auburn University sophomore and daughter Laura became an Auburn High School freshman.

On his selection as state superintendent of education in 1995, Dr. and Mrs. Richardson returned to Montgomery, where Nell continued her teaching career at Jefferson Davis High School. Dr. Richardson's contribution to public education in Alabama during his eight years as state superintendent of schools has been recognized as outstanding. He also contributed to the leadership of the boards on which he served, especially the AU Board of Trustees. In 1995, however, there was a bitter battle between the governor, who is ex officio president of the boards of public universities, and those board members whose terms on the AU board had expired. The fight was taken up by members of the Alabama senate, which has the power to approve or reject the governor's selections to the boards of trustees, and contention continued at Auburn until 1998, when Governor Fob James was replaced by Governor Don Siegleman.

At Auburn in 2001, Dr. Muse was replaced by Dr. Walker. The work of the trustee commission co-chaired by Drs. Richardson and Walker had been completed, and the Richardsons were both busy with their jobs and family. Early in the Siegleman administration a bill was brought before the legislature to remove the ex officio position of the state superintendent of education from the Auburn University Board of Trustees so that Auburn could offer more at-large positions on the board to out-of-state alumni. After many delays this was approved by the legislature; however, a measure to retain the state education superintendent's position on the Auburn board until the retirement or resignation of Superintendent Richardson was proposed and accepted. (The superintendent of Alabama's schools has continued to serve as ex officio member on the boards of many other state universities.)

There was a period of relative calm at Auburn University until December 2003, when a plane trip was taken by Dr. Walker, the athletic director, and two trustees to explore hiring a replacement for Auburn's head football coach. As Coach Tuberville had not been informed, the trip came in for widespread criticism, and the strong negative reaction forced Dr. Walker's resignation in early January 2004.

On January 17, 2004, Dr. Richardson's mother was celebrating her ninetieth birthday, but the celebration was offset by the appointment of Ed Richardson to the presidency at Auburn University. Dr. Richardson felt that he would need two or three years to clear AU of the probations it faced for violations in both university athletics and in administrative governance.

Although Mrs. Richardson had mixed emotions about her husband's sudden change of position, she knew that Dr. Richardson had wanted to see the Auburn University altered in a positive way that would redirect its land-grant mission and, hopefully, unify the Auburn University main campus with its namesake, AUM.

In the summer of 2004, Mrs. Richardson's love of home and family began to be redirected toward the historical home for the president at Auburn University. She found herself not only wanting to "fix up" the President's Home but also to write about the residence and its previous occupants. Among the first things she wanted to do was improve the grounds surrounding the home, and a first project was the repair of the old goldfish ponds in the front of the President's Home and in the formal garden area on the south side of the house.

Inside the house, Mrs. Richardson saw the need to continue the refurbishing and redecorating that Mrs. Walker had so ably begun. She also worked with Jann Swaim, head of special projects in the Facilities Department at AU, to add a new side porch off the sunroom and to remodel the small den.

When the Richardson's came to the President's Home in 2004, they had been associated with the city of Auburn and Auburn University directly and indirectly for forty-five years. They had known all the former occupants of the President's Home except the Duncans. Through a friend, Mrs. Richardson learned that Auburn historian and former columnist for the *Auburn Bulletin,* Ann Pearson, was the granddaughter of Dr. and Mrs. Duncan, and she contacted Ann. Ms. Pearson was interested in Mrs. Richardson's projects regarding AU's former first ladies and lent her support.

The Auburn football seasons of 2004, 2005, and 2006 were fabulous experiences for the Richardsons, who enjoyed greeting guests of Auburn University in the "sky box" president's suite at the home games and meeting the presidents and their wives from other Southeastern Conference universities at the bowl games and other events. During the 2004 season, the Auburn Tigers under Coach Tommy Tuberville, whose job had been in jeopardy in 2003, won every game and beat Virginia Tech at the Sugar Bowl in New Orleans. But 2005 brought some losses, and Auburn lost badly to Wisconsin at the Capitol One Bowl in Orlando. During the fall of 2006 the Tigers had their ups and downs, with wins that might have been losses and losses that should have been wins. The victory over Nebraska in the Dallas Cotton Bowl, however, seemed to quiet criticism of Tuberville.

At Auburn in every season and all year long, the air is filled with sports competitions and graduation ceremonies. Throughout their first year at Auburn, the Richardsons found their lives jammed with the social requirements of the presidency and with an exceptional workload as Dr. Richardson pushed to make the changes necessary for Auburn's removal from the probations placed upon the university by the Southern Association of Colleges and Schools (SACS) for lack of institutional control, and by the NCAA for rule violations that had placed the entire athletics program on probation until 2009.

In addition to the tasks associated with the removal of these sanctions and with the standard workload of the president's office, Dr. Richardson was faced with replacing several high-level administrators. Tension remained high on the Auburn campus, and life in the President's Home was strained.

In the legislative session of 2004, Dr. Richardson found that Auburn University had no plan for funding that could be presented to the state legislature. Having been aware of the recommendation made by the Alabama Commission of Higher Education in the early 1990s, Ed believed AU and the University of Alabama system needed to work together to move the state forward through higher education, and he worked to organize the Alabama Research Alliance, a partnership between the two universities.

For most of 2005 the Richardsons were also caught up in constant preparation for Auburn's sesquicentennial celebration, which added lots of extra fun and work throughout 2006. Committees met everywhere, and Mrs. Richardson joined the group that met monthly in the president's boardroom at Samford Hall. Many hours of careful planning went into preparations for the celebration of Auburn's 150 years of existence. When the birthday cake was served to all who came on the freezing-cold day of January 4, 2006, the lawn at Samford Hall was set up for the party that moved inside a tent. The day began with speeches, of course, and the warmth was extended by the heartwarming voices of the Auburn University Singers under the direction of Dr. Tom Smith, whose thirty-five-year career as head of the AU Choral Department ended with his 2006 retirement.

After the party, there was a walking tour of the almost completely pedestrian Auburn campus. It was led by actors dressed in period costumes and reenacting the roles of some of Auburn University's most outstanding historical figures, such as George Petrie, who was Auburn's treasured historian and author of the Auburn Creed as well as the writer of textbooks and the founder and coach of Auburn's first football team.

The sesquicentennial celebration seems to have involved every college and department. The Jule Collins Smith Museum decided to stage a first-ever "Art in Bloom" gala beginning on February 23, 2006. As a member of the museum committee, Mrs. Richardson met almost weekly with subcommittees.

In the Archives Department of the Ralph Brown Draughon Library, a lecture series was scheduled for Auburn's sesquicentennial celebration, and every month a lecture on some aspect of the university's history was presented. Mrs. Richardson was honored to be added to the list of well-published scholars, and on December 7, 2006, she presented the material she had gathered on the history of the President's Home.

The $500 million capital campaign for giving, known as "It Begins at Auburn," moved into high gear in 2006. On February 3 the campaign was officially launched at a black-tie gala affair set in a tent decorated in Auburn's orange and blue. It was a night to remember as the university launched the largest fund-raising effort in school history at the magically transformed John H. Watson Field House on Auburn's campus. The celebration gathered five hundred prominent alumni for the announcement that Auburn had succeeded in raising $332,472,021—two-thirds of the campaign goal. "Tonight's celebration was a great beginning of the public phase of our campaign," said Dr. Richardson. "With the momentum we have from last year's record fundraising and the enthusiasm evident tonight, I expect our campaign to be a tremendous success."[1]

This goal was reached before Dr. Richardson left Auburn on July 15, 2007. When the eighteenth president was hired for Auburn University in the spring of 2007, some of the changes President Richardson had made during his tenure were listed in the headline article of the *Birmingham News* on March 19, 2007:

> No change was more imperative than convincing SACS [the Southern Association of Colleges and Schools] that at Auburn the office of president had real authority, and trustees understood that their role was to set policy, not run programs. . . . [Richardson] fired a vice president, along with a longtime director of governmental affairs and the school's media relations director. He replaced the school's longtime athletics director and fired the head basketball and baseball coaches. . . . . He convinced trustees to adopt measures aimed at assuring SACS that the office of president was running the school, not the trustees. The board's long-standing and powerful athletics committee was disbanded, and an audit committee was set up to oversee a new trustee conflict-of-interest policy.[2]

On December 29, 2006, Dr. Richardson was honored by the Alabama Farmers Federation, a member of the American Farm Bureau Federation, and a summation of the speech he made at this event was featured in *Neighbors.* In an article titled "Back to the Land: Richardson's Vision for Auburn Brings New Look, Life to Agriculture," Ed spoke of his life as a teen on a small farm in southern Alabama and of the character of the hardworking people he knew there: "I watched people in Alabama . . . my family and others . . . just doing all they could do and doing without, just hanging on. . . . And I kept saying, 'What is it we can do? Are there niche markets out there? Are there different crops we can grow? What do we need to do?' [At Auburn] I talked with everybody . . . deans and presidents who had preceded me, and nobody really had much of an answer." He spoke of the great importance to agriculture and to the farm families of Alabama of Auburn's land-grant heritage, and said that the responsibility of the land-grant college "for educating Alabama's working class in agriculture and engineering" should be "redefined and repackaged in a way that is relevant to a changing world." Dr. Richardson expressed his belief that the establishment of an Institute of Natural Resources at Auburn would broaden "the definition of agriculture, and [play] a major role in solving the water, energy and environmental problems of the near future."[3]

In the President's Home in June 2007, Mrs. Richardson held her last social event as First Lady, a luncheon to celebrate the official unveiling of the portraits she had commissioned for the President's Home of the three First Ladies who presided over the home from 1939 until 1980: Mrs. Annie Duncan, Mrs. Caroline Draughon, and Mrs. Polly Philpott.

President and Mrs. Richardson at the sesquicentennial celebration on the plains, January 2006. (Auburn University Photographic Services)

Dr. Richardson with his mother, Doris, and granddaughter, Molly, in the president's suite at Jordan-Hare Stadium, 2004. (Auburn University Photographic Services)

Dr. Richardson taking suggestions from Auburn alumni on game day, 2005. (Auburn University Photographic Services)

A scholarship dinner for students and their parents, 2006. (Auburn University Photographic Services)

Open house at the President's Home, Christmas 2005. (Auburn University Photographic Services)

High tea for "Art in Bloom."
(Auburn University
Photographic Services)

Dr. Richardson in the center of the Women's Quadrangle with students of War Eagle Camp in 2005. (Auburn University Photographic Services)

In front of the William F. Nichols Center, President Richardson reviews the 2005 ROTC cadets at Auburn University's annual President's Review Day. (Auburn University Photographic Services)

"War Eagle" for Dean Foy's ninetieth birthday. (Auburn University Photographic Services)

Dinner in the President's Home for newly tenured faculty. (Auburn University Photographic Services)

On the field at Jordan-Hare Stadium in the fall of 2006, President Richardson with grandchildren Seth and Molly, their friends, and others, including Auburn's golden eagle mascot. (Auburn University Photographic Services)

Mrs. Richardson with Dr. Harry Philpott in front of Mrs. Polly Philpott's portrait at the official portrait unveiling luncheon in the President's Home, June 2007. (Auburn University Photographic Services)

The Richardsons with Ralph Draughon Jr. in front of Mrs. Caroline Draughon's portrait in the dining room of the President's Home, June 2007. (Auburn University Photographic Services)

At the portrait-unveiling luncheon in June 2007 in the President's Home, Dr. and Mrs. Richardson (*left*) are joined by Mrs. Cratus Bailey and her daughter-in-law, Wanda; Dr. Harry Philpott and his daughter, Jeanne, and daughter-in-law, Ann; Ann Pearson; Dr. Philpott's grandson, Britt; and Ralph Draughon Jr. (*right*) (Auburn University Photographic Services)

Gathering in the President's Home dining room for the portrait-unveiling luncheon in June 2007 are Mrs. Cratus Bailey, wife of Auburn's thirteenth president (*left front*), and Auburn's eleventh president, Dr. Harry Philpott (*head of table*), who is flanked by Ralph Draughon Jr. (son of Auburn's tenth president) and Ann Pearson (granddaughter of Auburn's ninth president, Luther Duncan). In the breakfast room behind archivists Dawayne Cox, Joyce Hicks, and John Varner is portrait artist Janice Ross. Across from Mrs. Bailey is dean of the Ralph Brown Draughon Library, Bonnie MacEwen. (Auburn University Photographic Services)

Notes

CHAPTER ONE

1. Mickey Logue and Jack Simms, *Auburn: A Pictorial History of the Loveliest Village,* rev. ed. (Auburn, 1996), 19.

2. Ibid., 25.

3. Joe Yeager and Gene Stevenson, *Inside Ag Hill: The People and Events That Shaped Auburn's Agricultural History from 1872 through 1999* (Chelsea, Mich.: Sheridan, 2000), 61.

4. Ibid., 510–11.

5. Eugene Davenport, *The Spirit of the Land-Grant Institutions* (1931), quoted in Charles Wesley Edwards, *Auburn Starts a Second Century* (Auburn: Alabama Polytechnic Institute, 1958), 12.

6. Edward Danforth Eddy Jr., *Colleges for Our Land and Time,* quoted in Edwards, *Auburn Starts a Second Century,* 13.

7. Malcolm McMillan and Allen Jones, *Through the Years* (Auburn: Auburn University, 1973), 6–7.

8. Yeager and Stevenson, *Inside Ag Hill,* 17.

9. Leah Rawls Atkins, *Blossoms Amid the Deep Verdure: A Century of Women at Auburn, 1892–1992* (Auburn, n.d.), 9.

10. Logue and Simms, *Auburn,* 64.

11. Yeager and Stevenson, *Inside Ag Hill,* 434.

12. Ibid., 29.

13. Ibid., 62.

14. Logue and Simms, *Auburn,* 40.

15. Yeager and Stevenson, *Inside Ag Hill,* 61.

16. Ibid., 81.

17. Caroline Draughon, notes on being inducted into The Mortar Board Honor Society at Auburn University, 1985, personal papers of Mrs. Caroline Draughon, Auburn, Alabama. An audio recording of Mrs. Draughon reading from her papers is kept in Special Collections and Archives at the Ralph B. Draughon Library in Auburn.

18. Ralph Draughon, "Christmas Letter to the Boys, 1943," Special Collections and Archives, Auburn University.

19. McMillan and Jones, *Through the Years,* 24.

20. Ralph Draughon Jr., "Recollections of the President's Home," 2006, possession of the author.

CHAPTER TWO

1. Kirtley Brown, "Huge Building Program Launched at Auburn," *Auburn Alumnus,* November–December 1938, 3.

2. Caroline Draughon notes.

3. Ralph Draughon Jr., "Recollections of the President's Home."

4. Ibid.

5. "Philpott Home Serves Notice That There Are Young People Around," *Lee County Bulletin,* May 12, 1966.

6. R. G. Millman, "Tour Four: The Windshield Tour," *The Auburn University Walking Tour Guide* (Tuscaloosa: University of Alabama Press, 1991), 82.

7. John Newton Baker, "Last Rites Held for API's President Luther N. Duncan," *Auburn Alumnus,* August 19, 1947, 2.

8. Ralph Draughon Jr., "Recollections of the President's Home."

9. Millman, "Tour Four," 82.

10. Redding Sugg, "Reporter Gives You a 'Look-See' at President's New 'Home on the Hill,'" *Auburn Plainsman,* October 8, 1940.

CHAPTER THREE

1. Edith Royster Judd, "The Homecoming of an Auburn Son," *Auburn Alumnus,* April–May, 1935.

2. Yeager and Stevenson, *Inside Ag Hill,* 73.

3. Judd, "The Homecoming of an Auburn Son."

4. Logue and Simms, *Auburn,* 127.

5. Ibid., 134, quoting from other sources.

6. Ann Pearson, "She Gave Silver Spoons," *Auburn Bulletin,* December 1978.

7. Yeager and Stevenson, *Inside Ag Hill,* 90.

8. Ralph Draughon Jr., "Recollections of the President's Home."

9. Pearson, "She Gave Silver Spoons."

10. Naomi Kirbo, "Lt. Duncan Feted at Farewell Dinner," *Lee County Bulletin,* May 23, 1942, 7.

11. John Newton Baker, "Last Rites Held for API's President Luther N. Duncan," *Auburn Alumnus,* August 19, 1947.

12. Ralph Brown Draughon, *Auburn Alumnus,* August 19, 1947.

13. Baker, "Last Rites."

CHAPTER FOUR

1. Leah Rawls Atkins, *Caroline Marshall Draughon* (Auburn: Craftmaster Printers, 1996), 9.

2. Martin T. Olliff, "The Post-War Years: Ralph Brown Draughon," Auburn University Digital Library, 1–4.

3. Atkins, *Caroline Marshall Draughon,* 11.

4. Caroline Draughon notes.

5. "Draughon to Be Inaugurated Today," *Auburn Plainsman,* May 12, 1949.

6. "Auburn's First Lady," *Auburn Alumnews,* October 1948.

7. Caroline Draughon notes.

8. Ralph Draughon Jr., "Recollections of the President's Home."

9. Ibid.

10. *Auburn Plainsman,* May 19, 1948.

11. Atkins, *Caroline Marshall Draughon,* 22–23.

12. Jacque Kochak, editor, *Auburn Villager,* August 30, 2007, interview with Leah Rawls Atkins on her soon-to-be-published centennial history of AuburnBank.

13. Caroline Draughon notes.

14. Logue and Simms, *Auburn,* 205.

15. Caroline Draughon notes.

16. Logue and Simms, *Auburn,* 201.
17. Olliff, "The Post War Years: Ralph Brown Draughon," 1–4.
18. Caroline Draughon notes.
19. Ralph Draughon Jr., "Recollections of the President's Home."
20. Olliff, "The Post War Years: Ralph Brown Draughon," 1–4.

CHAPTER FIVE

1. Dwayne Cox and Rodney J. Steward, "The New South," Auburn University Digital Library, 1–5.
2. "Florida Educator to Become Auburn President," *Alumnews Auburn,* May 12, 1965.
3. "Philpott Home Serves Notice That There Are Young People Around," *Lee County Bulletin,* May 12, 1966.
4. Karla Y. Davis, "The Post-War Years: Harry M. Philpott," Auburn University Digital Library.
5. Yeager and Stevenson, *Inside Ag Hill,* 515.
6. Ibid., 163.
7. Diane Townsend, e-mail to the author, 2006.
8. Royce Harrison, "Philpott Raps about the Pill, Parking, Drunks," *Auburn Plainsman,* May 14, 1971.
9. Logue and Simms, *Auburn,* 214.
10. Sarah Ramsey, "President's Wife Enjoys Civic, Campus Activities," *Auburn Plainsman,* May 8, 1975.
11. Ann Culbertson, "Harry Philpott: Gracious, Kind," *Auburn Bulletin,* August 31, 1975.
12. Caroline Nutter, Auburn University News Bureau, March 24, 1980.

CHAPTER SIX

1. Dave White, "Final Trustee Vote 10–1," *Auburn Plainsman,* April 8, 1980.
2. Grace Jones, "Mansion of Activities Face Helen Funderburk," *Auburn Bulletin,* September 14, 1980.
3. Ibid.
4. Helen Funderburk to Nell Richardson, April 6, 2006.
5. Ibid.
6. *Auburn Bulletin,* October 8, 1980.
7. Funderburk to Richardson, April 6, 2006.
8. Quoted in Yeager and Stevenson, *Inside Ag Hill,* 473.
9. Logue and Simms, *Auburn,* 305.
10. Marcia L. Boosinger, "The Post-War Years: Hanly Funderburk," Auburn University Digital Library.

CHAPTER SEVEN

1. Yeager and Stevenson, *Inside Ag Hill,* 28.
2. Ibid., 331–32.
3. Kate Bailey to the author, March 10, 2006.
4. Logue and Simms, *Auburn,* 292.
5. Bailey to the author, March 10, 2006.
6. *Auburn University News,* March 12, 1984.
7. "Dr. Wilford Bailey Passes Away," *College of Veterinary Medicine Newsletter,* 2000.

CHAPTER EIGHT

1. "What's behind the Man and Woman . . . Meet Ann and Jim Martin," *Auburn University Report,* April 2, 1984.

2. Kay Lovvorn, "Martin Pleased with AU," *Auburn Alumnews,* May 1984.

3. Logue and Simms, *Auburn,* 258.

4. Yeager and Stevenson, *Inside Ag Hill,* 503.

5. Ibid., 164.

6. "Martin Inauguration Set For Friday," *Auburn Bulletin,* April 25, 1984.

7. "Martins Bid Fond Farewell," *Auburn Alumnews,* March 1992.

CHAPTER NINE

1. Logue and Simms, *Auburn,* 292.

2. Auburn University Presidential Inaugural Special Section, *Montgomery Advertiser,* May 29, 1992.

3. Logue and Simms, *Auburn,* 263.

4. Yeager and Stevenson, *Inside Ag Hill,* 76.

5. Elma Bell, "AU's First Lady Takes Her Latest Move in Stride," *Birmingham News,* April 12, 1992, 1,3-E.

6. Logue and Simms, *Auburn,* 291.

7. Karen Kinnison, "Ablaze: 55-Year-Old President's Mansion Ignited by Maintenance Accident," *Auburn Plainsman,* May 5, 1994.

8. Jule Collins Smith Museum of Fine Art, History of the Museum, http://jcsm.auburn.edu/theMuseum/history.html.

9. Logue and Simms, *Auburn,* 288.

10. John Durham, "Muse Will Be Missed at Auburn, Looks Forward to ECU," *Pieces of Eight,* March 30, 2001.

11. Ibid.

CHAPTER TEN

1. Roy Summerford, *Auburn University News,* July 14, 1998.

2. Roy Summerford, *Auburn University News,* February 7, 2001.

3. William F. Walker, "Convocation," Auburn University, April 28, 2003.

4. Amanda Holmes, "President Hosts Welcome, Concert," *Auburn Plainsman,* August 22, 2003.

5. James Diffee, "First Lady of the Plains," *Auburn Plainsman,* October 16, 2003.

CHAPTER ELEVEN

1. "A Great Beginning," *Giving: It Begins at Auburn* (Auburn: Office of Communications and Marketing, 2006), 1, 4.

2. Charles J. Dean, "Who Will Lead Auburn?" *Birmingham News,* March 19, 2007.

3. Darryal Ray, "Back to the Land: Richardson's Vision for Auburn Brings New Look, Life to Agriculture," *Neighbors: A Publication of the Alabama Farmers Federation,* December 29, 2006.

Selected Bibliography

Atkins, Leah Rawls. *Blossoms Amid the Deep Verdure: A Century of Women at Auburn.* Auburn, n.d.

———. *Caroline Marshall Draughon.* Auburn: Craftmaster Printers, 1996.

Davenport, Eugene. *The Spirit of the Land-Grant Institutions.* Chicago, 1931.

Edwards, Charles Wesley. *Auburn Starts a Second Century.* Auburn: Alabama Polytechnic Institute, 1958.

Irvine, Paul. *Auburn's First 100 Years.* Auburn: Alabama Polytechnic Institute, 1956.

Logue, Mickey, and Jack Simms. *Auburn: A Pictorial History of the Loveliest Village.* Rev. ed. Auburn, 1996.

McMillan, Malcolm, and Allen Jones. *Through the Years.* Auburn: Auburn University, 1973.

Millman, R. G. *The Auburn University Walking Tour Guide.* Tuscaloosa: University of Alabama Press, 1991.

Yeager, Joe, and Gene Stevenson. *Inside Ag Hill: The People and Events That Shaped Auburn's Agricultural History from 1872 through 1999.* Chelsea, Mich.: Sheridan, 2000.